TO THE TOP
...without a glass

by
Ted "Lesk" Leszkiewicz

Warren Book Publishing Co.
P.O. Box 1376
Warren, Michigan 48090-1376

Published in the United States
by Warren Publishing Co.

All inquiries, orders should be addressed to:
WARREN BOOK PUBLISHING CO.
P.O. Box 1376, Warren, MI 48090-1376
ISBN—0—938287—00—1
Copyright Registration No. TXU 229-199
Library of Congress Catalog No. 86-50264
Title, To The Top Without A Glass.
1. Alcoholism — Rehabilitation — Autobiography
Book cover design by Ted "Lesk" Leszkiewicz
Collaborators/Editors: Drs. Ronald and Barbara Koscierzynski
First Edition

DEDICATION

To my wife ANN, the Florence Nightingale in my family, who nursed me back from near death many times . . .

To TED, PATRICIA, and GLORIA, my children, who stuck it out to the bitter end against many adversities . . .

To SUE LESZKIEWICZ and RUBY WEEKS for their prayers and support . . .

To ALCOHOLICS ANONYMOUS for guiding and supporting me through some rough times . . .

To AMVETS, the veterans organization that allowed me the privilege to go TO THE TOP — without a glass in my hand . . .

To DRS. RONALD and BARBARA KOSCIERZYNSKI, my collaborators and editors for all their help and support . . .

To ESSLEY BURDINE, for his legal counsel . . . To librarian BETTY CHIAVEROTTI, and assistant librarian PHYLLIS KALIN of the Warren Public Library for all of their help . . .

Most of all, TO THE SUPREME COMMANDER — without whom nothing is possible.

CONTENTS

Foreward

I was an alcoholic beginning with the first drink that I ever took. I swiped that drink from my father at the age of 15, together with one of his best cigars. From that moment on I had a drinking problem, but I didn't know it then.

For 32 years I drank progressively. In the process I lost a lucrative position as a field circulation manager with one of Detroit's largest newspapers, drank away two businesses, and put my marriage on the brink of disaster. At that point even my drinking buddies began to shun me. Finally, I saw the light. It was in the form of a candle, sitting on a table in the basement of my church during an Alcoholics Anonymous meeting.

This is my story — the story of an average guy's alcoholic experiences. I want to share my story with everyone, because the disease of alcoholism can strike anyone. Doctors, bankers, teachers, lawyers, ministers, sales people, factory workers ... alcoholism is a disease that does not discriminate by race, color, creed, sex, or occupation.

After total sobriety for over 20 years, I want to relate and share the joys of sobriety and the struggles to get there with all problem drinkers and recovering alcoholics.

Ted Leszkiewicz
Warren, Michigan

29 May 1986

Chapter 1

The Bottom and the Top

I hit my bottom in March 1962 when I had my last two week relapse from Alcoholics Anonymous (A.A.) under the apple tree in my back yard, fortifying myself with three bottles of wine. Until today I can not explain the phenomena that came over me momentarily, but I distinctly remember someone telling me that I may never have another chance to become totally sober again. So I took one more hefty swig, like a damn fool, and dumped the rest of the bottles behind the garage.

I just gazed into the sky above me for awhile after that, with many thoughts going through my mind. Like when I was a youngster and dreamed, as a lot of us do, about being a success at something. I didn't make it as a musician, artist, or as a newspaperman, or in any of my business careers. After all these years, I was still at the end of the line — a total failure and on the brink of disaster. I was an alcoholic . . .

I spent hours sitting there reassessing my whole life up to that point. It was the first time that I had really stopped and thought honestly about how I had selfishly wasted all those years and about what I had done to the people close to me. A complete inventory, and a complete turn-around. I finally LET GO and LET GOD.

The following week my mother and I attended a funeral for a friend of mine who was a veteran. My mother was very impressed with the beautiful military ceremony that he received. At that point she suggested that I should join a veterans organization so I could have a nice military burial when I died. That idea stuck in my mind. I had toyed around in my mind about joining such an organization since I was discharged from the U.S. Army some 17 years ago. I just had never found the time up to then to do so — I had been too busy — drinking.

In my neighborhood there was a post of the American Veterans of WWII, Korea, and Vietnam (AMVETS). I joined them, and I liked what I found. The drinking part did not bother me because I was searching for a new life of dedication. They had a huge number of service programs available to work on, and I got myself involved up to my eyeballs.

I must tell you at this point that I continued going to A.A. meetings morning, noon, and night for five solid years. I also attended services regularly at my church, since it was in their basement that I discovered A.A. in the first place. The secret to my sobriety from then on was to keep busy, busy, busy, instead of local bar-hopping. It worked for me, but I realize that it may not be the complete answer for everybody.

Little did I know at that time that my TOP would be with this special interest group. I set new goals and priorities for myself, getting involved in the Americanism, community affairs, and legislative programs of the Post. I also helped develop a nation-wide traffic safety program for high school students. In my spare time I "moved through the chairs," going from Post Commander to State Commander in a period of ten years.

I had my first major setback when I ran for a national office, that of National Executive Committeeman, and lost by six votes. That was the first time that I realized that credibility and reputation did not always win an election. Life in general is full of politics regardless of your career, school, church, or avocation. There is always victory in failure if you have learned something.

I refined my goals, resolved to get elected as National Commander in seven years. My first step was to get involved in the largest National District and be elected as its Commander. After the completion of the one year in that office, the National Finance Officer's position looked like a good next step for me in preparing myself for the top job. I ran for and was elected to that office for two years.

In 1977 a slot was available for the job of National Commander at the National Convention in Atlantic City, New Jersey. I was supported by a very strong group and had campaigned across the country for ten months. Up to the day before the election, it looked like I would be a winner.

At 3:30 in the morning we took a final head count and I was told that we had at least a 28 vote margin for sure. I also was told to go to bed so that the winning candidate would look fresh. It was an exciting morning of count down to the very end. The votes were cast, and again I lost by six votes. We had misjudged that we were in the opponent's home ground, and that a few undisclosed delegates could make a difference. Once again I had learned a lesson in defeat.

The spiritual communication and confidence that I had acquired from the members of A.A. and my Supreme Commander above were very strong. Such a major loss did not shake me up and drive me to take a drink after 16 years of sobriety. Instead, it motivated a tremendous desire to come back the following year and try again. Back in my home in Michigan, I sat down with my campaign manager, laid out new strategies, and restructured our planning committees in order to cover every segment of the country. We also developed an outstanding fund raising project for the coming year. I traveled extensively, especially in the enemy's camp, as they say politically. I admit that my job as a sign manufacturer and consultant/surveyor for a major automotive company made it easier for me to do so.

With a total of 133 hand picked delegates from Michigan and key people from around the country, each assigned with a specific duty, we went to the National Convention in Milwaukee and put on a campaign never before witnessed in that veterans organization. I won by a two-to-one margin. I had reached the top without a glass in my hand.

After taking the Oath of Office as National Commander, I left for Washington, D.C. to reside at National Headquarters. I will never forget the first time that I rode in the black limousine of Max Cleland, then head administrator of the Veterans Administration. It took me right into the White House grounds, where I was introduced to President Jimmy Carter in the Oval Office for a photo session. There were two more visits later to the White House, one of which was a beautiful luncheon followed by a discussion of the Salt II Treaty and other national security matters. There was always some reason to be on Capital Hill, but the most rewarding to me was presenting the AMVETS testimony to the members of the House and a separate speech to the Senate.

The delegates to the AMVETS National Convention in Milwaukee had mandated my administration to look for and build a new national headquarters building. We immediately put together an 18 man professional building committee, sold our old facility, and bought land in Maryland in a business/industrial complex 28 minutes from Washington, D.C. We then sat down with architects and builders and put together a real estate package for 23,500 sq. ft. new headquarters building that would cost over three million dollars. This was by far the biggest deal of my life!

During my year as National Commander we also organized a political action committee, developed a new nation-wide Veterans' Administration Volunteer Services (VAVS) program, and expanded our traffic safety "Driver-Excellence" program into 38 states. In between there was a continuous series of banquets and meetings in the finest hotels and restaurants with dignitaries of every level, foreign and domestic. I also traveled extensively throughout the United States visiting local AMVETS Posts and Departments. I received keys to many cities and made speeches to State Legislatures across the country. I was given resolutions, honors, and awards of all kinds. It is hard to believe that so much could be squeezed into so short a year.

My wife traveled with me quite a bit throughout the United States and to three foreign countries while I was National Commander. We were the guests of the Korean Government, where we spent ten fantastic days visiting various provinces. I think my wife got the best part of that trip. While I was busy attending meetings, she went shopping and visiting the points of interest in a private car with a personal guide.

While attending the World Veterans Federation Conference for 9 days in Paris, France, we were able to see quite a lot of the historical sites, including castles, mansions, and embassies. I even got to go to the top of the Eiffel Tower. What a beautiful view! Unfortunately it was too high for my wife. Our last foreign trip was to the Philippines for 15 days, where we visited such sites as Manila, Corregidor, and Baatan.

I finally felt that I had reached the TOP. The road to the top, however, had not been reached easily.

Chapter 2

Earlier Times

Both of my parents were born in Poland — my mother in Warsaw and my father on the Russian border in the village of Vilna. My father was the hard working laborer type and my mother was a typical housewife with an ability for business. Being of Polish heritage, they both had very strong Catholic beliefs and principles.

In 1913 my parents decided to move to the United States. After landing in New York City, they proceeded westward. They only got as far, however, as the Beaver Valley in the Alleghany Mountains near Pittsburgh, Pennsylvania. My father had found a job there as a laborer with the American Zinc and Chemical Company.

I was born in the town of Langloth, PA on January 14, 1916, the start of a family that eventually consisted of a brother and two sisters. I can remember Langloth as a town consisting of row houses with everything owned by the company. After three years there was a disastrous fire and the plant burned down to the ground. There was nothing left to do but pack up and get out of town. I visited there a few years back, and it is still more or less a ghost town.

We arrived in Beaver Falls, PA with a few hundred dollars and made a down payment on a dilapidated building that was once a grocery store with living quarters in the rear. After a few months of back-breaking cleaning and remodeling, my parents opened up the grocery store under the name of the Atlantic & Pacific Grocery Co. By working hard 18 hours a day, they were able to make a fair living.

Some of the earliest incidents of my youth are still etched in my mind. My father brought the art of making home brew with him from the old country. At the store there was a soda fountain section and you could buy any kind of ice cream your heart desired as long as you asked for vanilla. But my father had a steady stream of "preferred customers" who could get carry-out home brew.

Things were going along fine until Mrs. Green came into town and opened a candy store and ice cream parlor two doors away. Naturally some of my parents' business dropped off. By this time they had a little money saved up and decided to expand by bringing the business to peoples' doorsteps. They bought a Model-T Ford truck and built an open body so the merchandise could be displayed. My father then hit the road. He confined his route to a radius of 5 miles from the store because it was difficult in those days to climb steep hills with a heavy load. Many times he had to turn around and climb the steep grades in reverse gear. It gave a person a funny feeling to be driving down a hill and seeing a vehicle approaching in reverse.

I remember particularly the evening my first sister was being delivered by a mid-wife. In those days everything was hush-hush so they locked my brother and me in an empty room with only a tricycle and a kerosene lamp on a table. We discovered a little mouse in one corner so we put the table and lamp in the center of the room and started to chase the mouse around and around trying to run over him with my brother hanging on to me for dear life on the rear of the bike. My folks couldn't understand how we could be laughing so much in an empty room. We never could catch that mouse.

Another unforgettable event was my first day at kindergarten at the age of five. My mother walked with me to school, which was only about 10 blocks from home, and instructed me to wait for her after school. She was delayed enough to make me impatient and I proceeded on my own trying to remember how we got there. After a few blocks I zigged instead of zagging and after 20 minutes I crossed a bridge and found myself in Ambridge, a suburb. I began crying and finally somebody asked me where I lived. I recall telling them that my name is Ted Lesk (I couldn't spell the whole last name), I lived at 1015 Third Ave., and that we sold groceries and ice cream. I stopped before telling about the home brew part. I already knew that it was illegal. The nick-name Ted Lesk has stuck to me ever since. It also stuck with me never to zig whenever I should be zagging. Within a year after that the Great Atlantic & Pacific Grocery & Tea Co. chain store opened a mini-superette in town and my parents' grocery business declined very rapidly because of all that competition. They even sued us for infringement of their name use. I do not recall all the allegations and legalities but my folks got disgusted, sold the inventory and building, and moved southwest to a little town called New Cumberland in West Virginia.

In New Cumberland my father found a job in the coal mines, but he didn't like it very well. He was looking for another kind of livelihood and soon found a job as a construction worker. While employed in this capacity, he laid the original foundation to what is known today as the Weirton Steel Co., in Weirton, W. Va. This area is known as the upper panhandle. If a person stands at a particular point, they can have one foot in West Virginia, one foot in Pennsylvania, and throw a stone into Ohio.

We settled in Weirton and lived there for 18 years. After the construction of the tin mill was completed, my father got a job at the plant as a furnace-heater. What a hot job — he saved a lot of money on razor blades because the blast of heat from the furnace door kept burning off all his whiskers.

This was another town where everything revolved around the company, but at least everyone owned their own home. The company did not want outside labor representation and they formed their own company/employee association. To this day it is a giant in the steel industry without an outside labor union. The town grew and everyone prospered with it. It was here in Weirton that I began my career as a student.

Chapter 3

School Days

From the beginning of grade school I have fond memories of getting along with my teachers and fellow students, and of having no problem in getting above average grades. I entered the first grade at the age of six and showed exceptional interest in the violin. My basic studies of music began with a teacher named Mrs. Trimble in New Cumberland, W. Va. Every Saturday my lesson became an all day ritual because she lived about 12 miles away and buses didn't run very often. I studied under her tutorship for eight years until she couldn't teach me anymore. At that time I took advanced concert work with a teacher in Pittsburg, PA. This led me to the position of first violinist with the high school orchestra two years before I entered high school.

In the meantime, I had started to develop another new skill — art. I always managed to get a seat in the back where I was constantly drawing pictures with a book standing up to protect me from the eye of the teacher. Naturally, I was finally caught and moved up front. Even at the front of the room I still got away with murder because of my musical and artistic talents, forever doing something interesting for the class. I made all kinds of signs, classroom show-cards, and displays for the bulletin board, and I liked doing it.

During this time my musical career had advanced to being soloist at recitals, concerts with other orchestras in the area, and guest appearances on several radio stations. I also played at many banquets, wearing evening tails, always receiving accolades but no money. I recognized the fact that it takes many years of hard work and further advanced studies to be able to find gainful employment in a symphony orchestra or band. So I became discouraged with music and turned my interest more in the direction of art.

I had by this time researched the art works of many old artists and discovered that their talents weren't recognized until they were dead and buried. I therefore decided that commercial art was the way of the future for me. By studying graphic lettering I would be able to make some money by means of my artistic talents. I knew that I could never get married on what I was doing with my musical career. I had started to show an interest in girls and knew that I wouldn't like going through life as a bachelor.

At this point we had sold our home in town and bought a twenty acre farm. It was about four miles from town in an area known as King's Creek. We lived temporarily in a converted barn in the valley while my dad and the family were building a new house on the hillside. My father kept on working in the steel mill but started to raise chickens and set a goal of two thousand chickens to develop an egg farm. Everything went along beautifully until the bottom dropped out of the egg market and the cost of feeding all those chickens eventually put us out of business. We were eating chicken twenty-one times a week. It was a good thing we had a couple of cows to be able to drink milk because we had all lost all the desire for chicken alone.

I continued going to high school but my brother didn't like to study very much. He was more mechanically inclined toward machinery and electricity and always was repairing something. His genius became a tragedy after living in our hilltop house for two years. It was during the Christmas holidays that he was puttering around trying to fix an old kerosene stove that he had picked up. My mother had completed her washing and hung all the clothes in the basement to dry. My brother separated the clothes in the middle so he had room to work on his stove. Well, the stove got overheated and exploded amidst all those dry clothes and you know what happened. I was sitting in the living room above the fire, opened a window next to a new Zenith radio we had gotten for

Christmas and dropped it outside on the ground. There was a tall coat tree nearby that had all our new Christmas clothes hanging on it so I just picked up the whole thing and also threw it out of the window. Everything else burned and the loss was not completed covered by insurance. My brother tried to put the fire out by himself, but with a head start like that it was impossible to do anything to suppress it. He was burned badly himself and it almost became a total tragedy. He took it very seriously and spent many years with a guilty conscience before he got over it.

We moved back into the old barn down in the valley near the creek. The creek had an old swimming hole about 300 feet from the barn, and every once in a while the little creek would go on a rampage and wash out a wooden bridge that connected our farm to the main road. We finally built a steel girder bridge spanning the creek that eliminated future washouts.

Once again we started construction of a new house, this time in the valley that was only a foot above the grade of the creek level. In about 10 months my father and family completed a brand new two level house with hard wood floors and oak trim. This was all done in my father's spare time and weekends since he worked five and six days a week at the plant. It was a beautiful home and we lived very comfortably in it for about two years. Then the Monongehela and Allegheny Rivers in the Pittsburgh area went on a rampage after a severe storm. A few dams broke and flooded the Ohio Valley 30 miles south of Pittsburgh.

Well, you know what happened to our house. We had to flee to the hills with my mother being carried by my brother and me on our shoulders. After the flood receded from the second floor of our house to the point that we could get into the main floor, we began the immense task of cleaning up. What a mess! Our hardwood floors were twisted, turned, and ruined, but we made the best of it. How my father and mother were able to bear the cross, I do not know except that they had a strong belief in the Almighty that carried them through everything.

Chapter 4

My First Drink

In those days school was a full seven hour schedule from eight in the morning until three-thirty. A school bus picked us up at 7:00 a.m. at a spot on the country road and departed for home at four. If you missed the bus you had the "privilege" of walking. I walked the four miles many hundreds of times. No other transportation was available. I was always late for supper, using school as an excuse. By the time I usually arrived home, my brother had all the hard work done around the farm.

Many times I would stay overnight at my cousins' house as they lived in town. It used to worry my parents because we had no telephone to communicate. This happened quite often on Friday nights during basketball and football season. It was there that I was able to meet older people and I enjoyed their company.

My father still made his home brew and drank moderately over the weekends. Every two weeks, on pay days, my father always purchased a quart of whiskey and would stretch it out. I also experienced a lot of drinking going on in the older circle of people with whom I had started to associate, but I never took a drink myself. One day at the age of fifteen I swiped my first drink from my Dad's bottle, and one of his cigars. I liked it. I took another drink and gargled it in my mouth. It felt so mellow when I swallowed that one. That was the beginning of all my troubles, but I did not recognize it then — a real sign of danger.

My cousins had a boarder staying with them who was a heavy drinker and bought his supply in five gallon cans from a bootlegger. It was very easy to syphon off a pint from this large container and he didn't catch on. I also started to accept drinks occasionally from older people that I ran into. The desire to consume alcohol was getting stronger and I had to figure out ways to make money to buy liquor. It was during my junior year that I started to pay attention to girls more than to music. Even in those days we had what is known today as the "jet set". There were about eight of the best looking girls whose parents were from a business background and had a lot of money and drank freely. The only thing was that they preferred their company to be from amongst athletes, one of which I was not. That made me develop one more bad characteristic trait of resentment and I started to drink a little stronger — a sure sign leading to alcoholism.

At that time I received permission from the principal to open up a little sign studio back stage. Painting free displays for all the sports events gave me a lot of flexibility to make signs during certain class periods for local business people. I was, therefore, able to pursue my drinking habit.

My brother had also started to drink with two brothers whose parents owned a mini-superette market. The boys delivered groceries to phone customers and they always picked up a lot of money and had beer and wine in the delivery van all the time. This was a good source of drinking and went on for close to a year. The two brothers finally lost their lives in a horrible auto accident, both drunk and traveling over 100 mph. It was peculiar, but even at that early age, the only company we chose for ourselves was the drinking kind.

My senior year was a good one and I had my finger in nearly everything — except athletics. I had a God gifted talent for music and art but still wasn't satisfied. Graduation was a memorable occasion and I played my final violin solo "Thais" by Massanet, Opus No. V at the commencement exercises. I saw no financial future in music at that point and gave up the violin. For me, the graduation party turned out to be a four day drinking bout.

To digress and leap 50 years hence, I recently returned from my reunion of the class of 1933. It was an unforgettable experience and I am grateful to have lived that long. Out of a class of forty-eight, sixteen have passed away. I am very fortunate. Six of those who left this beautiful world died from alcoholism. The evening program was held at the exclusive Williams Country Club, consisting of a banquet and resume program. Almost all of my classmates had gone into the local steel mill and there wasn't much excitement in their lives. When it was my turn to tell my story, I spilled my guts just like it happened. Everyone listened in utter silence — you could hear a pin drop. There was a very warm response to my honest testimony and so many comments afterward that made me feel very good to have let it out.

Going back to the farm life after graduation was not pleasant for me, so I talked my parents into sending me to college. I hated farm life. I finally convinced them and they decided that a geographical change might improve my life-style from drinking. I was off to St. Mary's College in Orchard Lake, Michigan, which is a Catholic seminary. Looking around me, I immediately could see that the discipline was too strict for me and my preparation to study for priesthood would never work out. In six months time, I got involved in some pranks, and my drinking problem showed up immediately. The monsignor tried to talk to me, but to no avail. I did make a good friend out of the psychology professor who could understand my problems. I met him twenty-five years later at an AA meeting. What a small world!

I wrote my parents a letter saying that I could not continue my studies there and if they didn't get me out I would jump from the third floor and commit suicide. There was an art school called the Detroit School of Lettering that I was reading about and I told my folks I would like to attend and that I could live at my uncle's place in Detroit which was only 28 miles away. My parents talked by telephone with my uncle about this arrangement, and he agreed to it. I quit college before being expelled. Fortunately for a lot of congregations, I did not become a priest.

Chapter 5

Career Development

My uncle had a very good job with an automobile manufacturer. He had a son and a daughter a little younger than me. I enrolled at the art school for evening classes so I could do part time work to pay my way. I discovered that my uncle supplemented his income by making booze in the bathroom. He kept it stored in gallon jugs and in five gallon tin cans. You can imagine what a glorious heaven I found for myself. I soon had many new friends in the neighborhood with whom to share my discovery. My uncle's business dropped off considerably because I gave it away.

When my uncle left for a weekend, we really had a bash. I even convinced my cousins to join me. This went on for about eight months. In the meantime, I became impatient with the school because they kept me so long on lettering the ABCs and I already had that knowledge a long time ago. My aunt finally discovered the party episodes when we left some telltale marks of white rings from whiskey glasses on her piano. After my liquor supply was cut off, I left my uncle rather than causing any further embarrassment.

Upon returning home, I landed a job at the G.J. Murphy Company for three months. Then I got grandoise ideas about becoming a business man. I rented a small empty store with borrowed money and set up a sign shop. I did very well and my drinking capacity increased. There was a large moving and storage outfit in town that needed lettering on two new large vans. I did this work for the owner, but it took him a long time to pay his bill. In the meantime, we became very close friends even though he was over ten years older than me. This worked out for me because he knew all the contacts I needed to expand my clientele and, more so, he knew all the nice places to go. He accepted me as a drinking partner and we frequented all the nice nightclubs in Wheeling, West Virginia; Stuebenville, Ohio; and the Pittsburgh, Pennsylvania areas.

Not realizing then that drinking had already become a problem with me, I worked all day so that I could drink all night with my older friends. Business improved. Before long, I was painting signs and shocards for a five store shoe chain, and trimming windows for our local department store. While trimming a window at the jewelry store one evening, a beautiful young lady accompanied by two small children pulled up to admire the merchandise. Upon asking the owner who the girl was, he remarked that I couldn't get next to her with a ten foot pole and should not waste time thinking about her. This then, became my first major challenge.

After a little research, I discovered that she worked for a local doctor and also that my father and hers were old friends. So I pursued to lay my strategy to make her acquaintance. Calling her on the phone at the doctor's office did not work and I couldn't make a date with her with that approach. So the con artist that an alcoholic is, I showed up at her house and brought a gift of a pint of Canadian whiskey to offer to her father. I introduced myself, brought greetings from my dad, and proceeded into a very intimate conversation. After about an hour of acting the role of a real gentleman, I told him how I saw his daughter in the jewelry store a few weeks ago. He called for her to come out to the back porch to meet me. She had, however, overhead us discussing her and she had left the house.

Not giving up that easily, I came back the following Saturday night with another bottle of whiskey and a lot of conversation. I sold myself to his confidence. I had a little money saved up and bought a 1933 DeSoto convertible with jumbo tires. That was "it" in those days. After a few visits, her father finally convinced his daughter Ann to come out and meet me. That was the beginning of a beautiful romance. Little did she know about my drinking problem which would bring her so much grief later. I kept my heavy drinking pattern away from her by restraining myself even though the local business merchants had made some remarks to her about my life style. Fortunately for me, she did not believe them at the time. Business flourished, and within two years I had both sides of Main Street painted up and soon I would be out of business. By this time my parents had sold our farm and moved back into town.

While my dad continued working at the steel mill, an outside union, the United Steel Workers (USW), had opened a local office in an effort to organize the workers. Out of curiosity, my mother attended one of their meetings. Before you knew it, the word got out and my father was fired with a seniority of nineteen years.

In 1936, after bidding my future wife goodbye, I left town with my brother to seek our fortunes in Detroit. Fortunately, there were jobs available at the Chrysler/DeSoto automobile plant on Jefferson Avenue. I was able to work there for three months. After that experience, I promised myself never to go back to a production job in an auto plant. My brother and I got a job at a real estate sign company and wrote back home to have our father join us in this great big city of opportunities. I thought this geographic change would help me with my drinking habit. It only progressed to a greater degree. I brought the problem with me to a new environment, and it thrived.

Chapter 6

Then She Said "Yes"

The work at the sign studio slowed down because of the depressive economy and we were out looking for employment in a very short time. My father and brother were hired by a stoker furnace company. Moving around, I managed to get placed as a layout sign writer with Chevrolet Art and Display Division. This looked like a bright future. I called up my girlfriend Ann and conned her into coming to Detroit. Little did she know what her dreams were to reveal. We were married on September 7, 1937 at the height of the depression. Things were very tough in the City of Detroit, but I managed to work many hours of overtime, largely because it was the season of automobile shows.

The pattern of alcoholism continued. I couldn't stand the prosperity. My ego was inflated from the newly found success and the bars were doing a brisk business every night during my visits. What a miserable life for a new wife! She left a job and the security of her father's home to wind up with a heavy drinking husband for a lifetime. She certainly exhibited a lot of courage and patience.

My father bought a three family brick flat on the east side and we all lived together. I didn't miss any days from work due to my heavy drinking at night. The work at the display department fascinated me and I was intrigued with its creativity. In a very short time, my job allowed me to design, make layouts, full size patterns, and do sketch work. This was a terrific experience for me. The signs, banners, and displays that we built were shipped all over the country. Sometimes I would go to the General Motors Headquarters Building where they would all be on exhibit on the main floor and literally become immersed in the displays. A new and exciting world was there for me. During the automobile show, then held at the state fair grounds, we would work around the clock. Sometimes we would get only about four hours of sleep. Instead of going home, we would sleep on piled up drapes, velour material, or on whatever else was handy. The money was terrific, but I managed to save very little because of my heavy drinking.

Our first daughter, Patricia, was born at home because we couldn't afford the hospital. The home delivery of that new baby will be a lifetime memory. I was at the doctor's side with my mother assisting during the entire time. After it was all over, I remember downing almost a whole pint of whiskey and then passing out.

My newly found opportunities with the display business petered out after about seven months. Conditions around Detroit were hitting the bottom and my father and brother both lost their jobs at the stoker company. We all hit the pavement again looking for employment. Things got very bad and our two tenants were behind in their rent. We went to the welfare office for assistance. They told my father that he was too "property rich" for help. He was advised to sell the property and live on the proceeds. Our tenants were able to get some groceries and coal. They gave us a bag of oranges to carry us over. We all felt extremely depressed.

Luckily, my father found a job as a sand blaster at the foundry four blocks from home. A new sense of confidence and enthusiasm came to us. My brother became an electrician's helper and I got a position as an apprentice helper for the Long Sign Company. They specialized in the manufacture of theater signs and marquees.

My job now was on the road repainting high structures. I recall working the first day on the old Hollywood Theater's vertical sign. It was over twenty stories high above the sidewalk. The wind was blowing about thirty miles an hour and I was swinging from a chair. Everytime I swung past the face of the sign, I would dab it with paint. The next day I found out how to hold myself in place with

outstretched legs. My journeyman boss thought it
was a big joke. We got along pretty well because he
also liked his "schnapps".

We would start on a Monday morning at the shop.
After loading up the truck with a week's supply of
paint and orders, we would hit the road. We were
mostly our own bosses, and could therefore take
advantage of certain situations. On Fridays the owner
would bring our paychecks to the job.

We had several interesting incidents, but one is still
etched in my mind. We had been working for three
days on a wall job for a tailor. Dan, my straw boss, got
thirsty around 11:00 a.m. It was a hot day. He
instructed me to fill in the large letters which he had
outlined. This sign happened to be on the outside
wall of the fifth floor of a building on Woodward
Avenue and I was enjoying looking at the traffic view
below. Looking carefully at the big letters, I changed
the shade of the color. Around 2:00 o'clock, the
owner pulled up with our paychecks. He took one
look at the background color and called me down.
First he asked me where Dan, the straw boss, had
gone to. I covered for Dan and quickly explained that
we had run out of turpentine. The owner was a
Christian Scientist and he did not approve of alcohol
consumption. He accepted my excuse for Dan's
absence.

He then asked me who selected the color for the
letters. I explained to him that the color I had mixed
would look better. He made me climb up the five
floors with the stage and bring down the colored
sketch that served as our guideline. He told me, in no

uncertain terms, that I wasn't paid for thinking, only for painting. Even if the sketch blows off the roof, follow it. I came back on Saturday on my own time to change the color. He did give me Dan's check, but I didn't get mine until Monday.

Soon Dan and I were getting pretty chummy. He was the representative of the local signwriters union and had a lot of seniority. This place was very busy during the summer because of repaints of theaters on a maintenance contract. I wished to work the inside during the winter months so that I could learn a little bit about custom built neon signs. That wish, however, never came true. They had to let me go just before Christmas because I had brought in a bottle to toast everyone. There were no excuses that could keep me there. Once more I became very resentful. It led me to heavier drinking.

Chapter 7

Big Business Man

I was "snapping" signs in grocery stores and gas stations to keep going. Finally connecting with a tire store chain for some work, we were able to buy a new stove, refrigerator, and some furniture. Like a typical alcoholic, the only friends I could meet were in a bar. Naturally, I started to repaint all the bars in the Grand Boulevard/Gratiot area. I opened up a sign shop in my basement and TED LESK & CO. was launched. There was plenty of business for me at the five gas station/appliance stores. I was living high and by now owned an old car. I was able to reach out to more bars and do their painting and remodeling. They liked me because of the money that I spent there each night. No one objected to my drinking and I was in my glory.

Most of my bar work was done during the daytime. I usually collected for my work at night because that was when the owners were there. It fitted into my "stinkin-thinkin" well. One evening I was in a bar waiting for the boss to come in. I had done some neon repair work in his window. This nice bar was located across the street from a newspaper sub-station. At midnight, these circulation distributors, about six in this territory, would walk in. They all had money bags from collections of paper stands, corners, and home delivery boys. This fascinated me to the point that I came back the next night. I spent the next two weeks getting acquainted with the boss. He seemed to be a jovial type of guy and we immediately struck up a friendship. Besides, he and all the other distributors drank.

I had observed that newspaper people seemed to be two-fisted drinkers. Boy, that was sure my style. Scotty Bright, the boss, asked me if I could make a city-wide map for him. Going along with the experience that I told him I had at Chevrolet's, we agreed on a contract to build a ten foot by twenty foot map. It was to be wired showing every corner, route, and sub-station in the city. Like a good drinking braggart, I told him it would be no problem to make such a sign. Well, when I sobered up the next day, I realized then what I had gotten into for a $700 fee. That was big money in 1939. However, background materials and electrical components for this project were also expensive. The map was constructed in five sections of treated ¾ inch plywood. I had to do a lot of research to get the right kind of map and to have it blown up to fit. Attaching it permanently to the background was also difficult. I outlined everything in color-coded lines as specified. Being in five sections made it difficult to wire. My brother saved me on this one. We put it all together in a two car garage which I had rented.

That night we really broke a bottle of champagne celebrating. All was well until we got the sign to the Detroit Free Press Building. Getting off on the fifth floor at the circulation department, I discovered that the map would not go through the doorways turning into the main room. So it was back to my garage to cut the map in half. The whole thing then had to be rewired because of the cut sections. After a week, the map was completed and the top circulation manager was very pleased. Scott, the district man, knew that I had lost money on the deal and felt obligated. From the minute I had met him, I had my eye on a district sub-station manager's job. They all drove nice cars and had a bag full of money all of the time. Best of all — drinking was acceptable. This was what I was looking for all my life, or so I thought.

To help me out, Scotty did some maneuvering with the hierarchy downtown and created a new district on the far eastside. I became a new field circulation manager at $45.00 a week. I was thrilled. The only bad part about this job was that it was night work, supposedly from 8:00 p.m. to around 1:00 a.m. It was a seven day a week job and they allowed me so much for car expenses.

My wife objected at first because she could see that the night work was no good for me. Explaining to her that working nights would permit me to continue my sign business during the day, she finally gave in against her better judgment. A newspaper career was started. The first six months I behaved rather well and bought a new car. They put me on a bonus plan of increasing my home delivery sales and I ran with it. I was always very ambitious in whatever I touched. Before long, I was making $75.00 a week in bonuses.

We finally moved out of my parents' home and got a beautiful two family home near my new territory. The job suited me "to a T" but I just couldn't control my drinking after I got started. Some of the single fellows in my district were running around and the night life appealed to me. Soon I was unable to do as much work during the day as I had previously projected. My day business fell off completely in a couple of years. It seemed that after I closed the bars every night, I wound up in speakeasies either downtown or in Mt. Clemens. My boss always reminded me not to do as he did, but to do as he told me.

I could not understand why my bar buddies could stop drinking when they wanted to and why I couldn't. Already I was over the line and a victim of alcoholism. I did not understand that it was a disease and kept on fighting it. I wouldn't admit to myself that I was a total failure at social drinking. It was a sickness with me. But I managed to progress fairly well in my newspaper job.

By this time we had three children. The youngest,

my boy Ted, was only six months old when I received my draft notice. I was to report for induction into the U.S. Army in thirty days. I couldn't believe they were scraping the bottom of the barrel because I was over the age limit of twenty-six. None of my close relatives had gone into the service, and I really developed a case of self-pity.

Final arrangements had to be made at the newspaper for my leaving for the service. They were good enough to give my wife half of my take-home pay while I was gone and it helped to take care of her and my children. There was also a few thousand dollars in the bank. A night club which I had extensively remodeled owed me about $4000. The owner was paying my wife $200 a month on the balance.

There wasn't one sober day until I reported to Fort Sheridan, Illinois in December 1944. I was assigned to the United States Army Corps of Engineers.

Chapter 8

Private Engineer

Basic training is no push-over. For me, however, it was even worse because my physical condition was not the best from excessive drinking. The push-ups were killing me and for two weeks the booze was pouring out. This was a new ballgame for me and it was hard to adapt to the new authority and restrictions. Drying out was especially tough. I had passed my physical with flat feet, so the five and ten mile marches were landing me in the hospital. In spite of all my complaining of not being able to walk or march, they merely kept on changing my shoes and socks. I finally realized I had to live with it and decided to adjust to Army life.

There was always a crap game going on at night after the lights were out. One fellow from New Jersey was doing all the banking because he always had a roll. Staying up all night made a person sleepy all day. This fellow had developed certain tactics that he put to his own use. He trusted me and shared some of his "secrets" with me. On night marches he would be behind me with his finger tips on my shoulder. Ted, he said, don't break the rhythm of your march. That way he could doze while marching. When we stopped for a five minute break he would hit the ground. He would be snoring in forty seconds. One day I asked him how he was able to do that. He explained that there was nothing to it but concentration. Close your eyes like a venetian blind and lock everything out. I developed that habit before I left the army.

One day we were in the woods on a water filtration exercise. The first "looey" had us standing in a semi-circle while he explained the exercise. Good old sleepy Sam was standing next to me. He was leaning against a tree at a sixty degree angle. In forty seconds he was snoring. The lieutenant finally walked up to him and waved a hand across his seemingly open eyes. Sam didn't even move. The officer pushed his leaning arm and Sam almost wound up with a busted eardrum that day. From then on, Sam was a bit more careful.

Out of a contingency of twenty-three thousand men, I ran across a man from Cheboygan, Michigan. We both had the same MO number and both were assigned the job of lettering names on helmets. This job entailed painting half inch letters with a delicate brush. The skin on our fingers was peeling off from the GI soap and in three days we were excused from future kitchen duty. I made the sergeant a beautiful desk name plate and we got along quite well after that.

Being confined to the post for six weeks during basic training was no picnic. It didn't take too long to figure out a way to have whiskey brought in. Like anything else on the sly, a little extra money and connections were part of the right formula. I should have recognized then that I had a serious problem. After the first drink, the next twenty didn't make any difference until I passed out. We kept our adventure undercover and never drank during the day.

After six weeks of basic combat training were completed, we were shipped out in all directions. A train load of us pulled into Fort Belvoir, Virginia for further training. The camp was located nineteen miles southwest of Washington, D.C. I was assigned to the headquarters company and that was pretty good living. We continued our specialized training in bridge building, heavy construction equipment for road building, and communications. I specialized in my own talent of sign painting and taught a class of sign writing by the numbers. They took civilian truck drivers and made cooks out of them and vice versa. I did my duty as assigned and was left pretty much alone.

The old saying that "it takes one to know one" happened to me very quickly. I met Frank, the youngest son of a wealthy oil family from Pennsylvania. He had three other brothers in the army. All of Frank's brothers had attained a high rank. One was a brigadier general, one was a colonel, and the third was a major. Frank was a mere private - by choice. He wouldn't accept a commission to go to OCS. He liked it this way. He liked to drink. We took a liking to each other and became good buddies. After our duties were completed on Friday, we took the post taxi into Washington, D.C. for the weekend. To me, this city was the eighth wonder of the world. I spent a lot of time visiting everything.

Frank liked to travel a lot but did not like to drive. His family set up an account at the Mayflower Hotel where he could draw $25 per day to carry him over. What a beautiful arrangement. Our problem was transportation. I told Frank about my nice two-tone 1940 Plymouth coupe which I had left at home. We made a deal. I would furnish the transportation while he would supply the money for our pleasures. One stipulation was that we would be back in time for reveille call every morning.

After a week of communication by telephone with Ann about bringing the car to the post for transportation, she finally agreed. There was no problem getting gas ration stamps or a tire allowance. Everything was available on the post. Our usual daily pattern consisted of going to D.C. after a day of working at the post. I would supplement my car money by stopping at the taxi stand to pick up passengers at a dollar a head for the trip. They would practically break the hinges off the car door. The revenue going in would more than pay for all the gasoline plus a bottle of whiskey for the next day.

Our first step was the hotel to pick up Frank's allowance. Then we would go to the Trans-Lux theater restaurant for a classy dinner. The evenings would be spent bar hopping. However, I had to restrict my consumption because I was the driver. This was quite a handicap. Usually by midnight we managed to close out the bar at which we were. I would lay down in the back seat of the car from 1:30 to 2:30 a.m. for a rest and then was able to drive back to camp. On the way back we again stopped in the taxi line for three soldiers, again picking up a few extra bucks.

I couldn't keep up with Frank's generosity and convinced my wife to send me $1500 with which to open a post account. I told her the car had developed some major problems and I needed new tires. Well, you know where the money went. During the war, whiskey was rationed in all the states except in the District of Columbia. It was easy to get a trunkful without any problems. That's exactly what I did every other month before I would visit my family in Detroit. There was a $500 profit on every trip and I would give my wife a "C" note. She thought that was really great. I made myself a big man. Again the ego blew up. The characteristic traits of alcoholism kept creeping up but I didn't want to see them.

Around 1945 my company of nineteen men was assigned to a special duty. We were beginning a major project in a secluded warehouse on the old post. The officer in charge was a first lieutenant from New York City. He had come from a large advertising agency and was very knowledgeable about model making and displays. That was right up my alley and I was promoted to corporal. We worked together very well and I was so interested in my new assignment that I even curbed my drinking in half.

To briefly explain, we made scaled models of everything we could find from a blown-up aerial photograph. The final assembly was constructed of twenty-five sections and it stretched out over two hundred feet in length in the warehouse. The bad part was being confined to the post for an eight week period. No more weekend sprees. But I soon figured that one out as well. I told my lieutenant that there were two artist supply stores which I used to visit on my trips into town.

He assigned me his personal jeep which I could use for procuring materials at least twice a week. That gave me a few hours for myself and I brought the whiskey back in a turpentine can. He would also take a nip every once in a while. I also made some special visits to the Pentagon. Although they were shipping men overseas every month, I felt I was making my contribution as a specialist. I was doing a significant job. During this special construction period, I became acquainted with the commanding general of the post. He later assigned me to one of his pet projects. After we completed our project and shipped it to the Pentagon, we each received a ten day furlough and I was pulled off of overseas shipment twice. The war was coming to a close and I had over forty points accumulated, making me eligible for discharge.

An interesting event happened to me at this time. I had been working on a four foot by eight foot display for the commanding general's office. This display depicted all the training areas and buildings on the entire facility. I found out that a full colonel from my home town had come on the base on vacation. I went to visit him at the officers' quarters and it was nice to go back a few years. He asked me how my Polish was and I said that it was terrific. Little did I know what he was planning. He was to go back to Poland after two months of rest. Outside of Warsaw, they were to establish a camp for Polish displaced women. He couldn't speak the native language very well and wanted me to be his interpreter. This duty was a minimum of two years and I already had enough points to get out.

Imagine me, the only American soldier other than him, speaking the Polish language. I would have killed myself if I could not fall back on my drinking. The colonel had me put on shipping orders to leave the following week. I scampered around in a great hurry. Getting all my gear together for shipment, I contacted the commanding general and told him that I would be unable to finish his beautiful wall display.

In a few days I was on the troop train pulling out of camp. A jeep pulled out in front of the train while the engineer was blowing his whistle. Talk about sweating it out! The general had me pulled off that shipment and the colonel never forgave me for that. To kill time until our discharge, we completed a historical museum of the entire post and I finished my special display and received a special citation.

I was honorably discharged from the army in December 1945 with forty-five points and thus ended another brilliant drinking career.

Chapter 9

Civilian Ted

It didn't take long to adjust myself to civilian life. Instead of being grateful that I came back alive and all in one piece, I still had a bad resentment. This is just another crutch on which an alcoholic learns to lean. Just another excuse to drink more.

Prior to the service, I had put together the format of a machine-tool enterprise. I already had the contacts to obtain the necessary government contracts. Selfishness and jealousy made it hard for me to get along even with my relatives. None of them had gone into the service. I drove myself back into heavy drinking with this attitude.

After about two weeks out of uniform, I went back

to my old job at the newspaper. To show my appreciation to the newspaper for their goodness to my family while I was in the service, I applied myself very hard. I changed my style of drinking to periodic bouts rather than my previous pattern of daily drinking. Working very hard in my home delivery area, it soon doubled in circulation. My compensation was equal to the second highest paid district in the whole city.

Putting my daytime sign business back together was rather difficult. A shortage of steel, wire, and all other related materials kept me from growing to my former peak of production. I was very short of cash so my brother-in-law joined in as a partner. This arrangement was a good one for both of us. He also had a station manager's job with the newspaper with a territory bordering mine. He was a very nice person and a family man. We could work side by side. My wife and his wife were also very compatible.

With an influx of new cash, I suggested opening up a new type of party store. This idea came to me while I was in the service on one of my visits to Baltimore, MD. The front end of the store was strictly a classy display area for fine wine and liqueur. On the side walls there was a huge selection of domestic and imported canned foods. Some of the prices were so high you would think they came overseas by rowboat.

We were located in an exclusive area of the eastside near the Pointe. There was no problem getting a good mark-up on the merchandise. Best of all, it was a good source of getting drinks for myself at a wholesale rate. This operation took many hours of our time and the delivery system we had spoiled our customers. They would accumulate four to six cases of empty bottles and call us. We would refund the cash for the empties. That practice helped break the camel's back in profit. We finally sold the place and were lucky because we doubled our investment. Upon splitting the profits, my brother-in-law bought a cottage on Harsen's Island. I blew my share of the money in a very short time.

At this time we were living with my folks again on the near eastside and I continued my periodic escapades. I had been warned several times about my excessive drinking, but an alcoholic doesn't scare easily. The third time was the real "carpet" treatment. The Teamsters Union to which I belonged tried to talk some sense into me. The newspaper offered to send me to an alcohohic treatment center in Kentucky for a six month period. What did I tell them? Who — me??? I drink with the rest of them around here.

Drinking with the others was alright they said. But they impressed on me that I didn't know when to stop. An AA man got hold of me and tried in every way to help me. Even my minister from the Lutheran Church tried to counsel me, but to no avail. I attended one AA meeting and laughed at those guys around the table. I started to compare myself to them. I was no bum. I was earning $200.00 a week. I was a somebody. Well, there is an old saying around AA that if you join them to save your job or your marriage it won't work out. It didn't, and I really hit the skids in sorrow and in self pity.

At first, conditions at home were pretty normal

because there was still a little cash left. Staying with
my parents helped because the rent was nominal. My
wife was consoled by my mother. I stayed away from
home days at a time. It was not a good family
atmosphere. While still working at the press, my
reputation was still solid as a good spender. When I
became short of cash it was no problem to borrow
hundreds of dollars at first. At one particular bar, the
owner took a liking to me. I was short and asked
Louie for $500.00. He gladly gave it to me and even
asked if that was enough. I told him that it would be
paid back in thirty days and it was. Well, the next
bundle of money that I borrowed from him took ten
years to repay. What made it worse was that I did not
go there again for a long time.

I was known as a first class salesman in my
neighborhood. Standard equipment in my own car
included a nice briefcase, army blanket, and a pillow.
Leaving the house every morning dressed
immaculately, my wife thought I was out selling
signs. It worked for a long time. I would visit about a
half dozen different bars every day and have two
drinks at each one. Then I would leave. They would
say to themselves, now there's a real salesman — he
knows his limit. What they didn't know was that I
would drink myself into a stupor at an off-street place.

This type of living grew on me and I was really
enjoying myself again. I always drove a nice Buick car
and wore expensive clothes. Every morning two
dollars of gas went into the car so I could travel from
place to place. Every once in a while I would sell a sign
and pick up a few hundred dollars. My wife would be

lucky to get a twenty dollar bill out of me.

I was very good at designing and sketching on the spot. I would engage in a conversation with the owner of a bar or restaurant and immediately made a rough colored pencil sketch with pastel overlays. Most of the time I was able to walk out with an order and a sizeable deposit. Previous connections from my good old days had these orders built and installed. I only designed, sold, and handled the cash — a really good deal for a drinking man.

As I said, my drinking pattern had changed to periodic bouts and things moved along, but abnormally. A four to six week bender became my limit. Then the old bills would be caught up and my car got out of hock. The finance company owner became a very good friend of mine and helped me in tight spots. The last two $500.00 loans he gave me were personal ones without interest. I thought I was really living. My problems, however, became bigger when I sobered up. I was acquainted with a lot of policemen from my newspaper days. They would pull me over once in a while and would try talking to me. Someday it would be the wrong cop and I would be sorry.

One incident happened on Harsen's Island while driving home stinko from the San Souci Tavern. I was weaving down the road bordering the river and veered off the road, almost plunging into the water. With my luck, the local police pulled up and I couldn't even get out of the car. They took me into Port Huron and threw me into the drunk tank. That really insulted my intelligence. Imagine being thrown in with a bunch of drunks. Besides, I had shorts on and all night I was backing up into a corner for protection.

The authories had notified my wife and my court case came up in the morning. The judge fined me $75.00 and gave me a warning about taking away my license for six months. You would think this would scare me into being more careful about my drinking. However, after that I did take the advice of my Detroit police friends and went to sleep in the back seat after excessiveness. That was where the briefcase, pillow, and blanket came in handy all year long.

Chapter 10

Adventures of Citizen Ted

Those of you who spend a lot of time in bars know the kind of people who live there day and night. Nice family men who can control their amount of intake, problem drinkers, drunks, con-men, numbers men, etc. It's a good place to meet them all. It seemed that was the only kind of acquaintance that was comfortable to me.

One day I met a man near my home tavern who was really loaded with money. After a few days we began to share our lifestyle of drinking and I never bothered to ask him about his source of income. I did find out later that he had recently sold his bar. But what did I care ... He spent money like water and seemed to know the right kind of people, or so I thought.

He had a friend who owned a men's clothing store a block from my house. There was a lot of traffic coming in and out of his clothing store. Very few people, however, were carrying out any garments. I found out later that it was a main numbers pick-up station. He had a big man who was his right hand and bodyguard. The four of us became really good drinking buddies. During the first eight months of our association, the true background of my buddies was unknown to me. In the neighborhood we were called the "Big Four". I didn't care. The drinks were pouring. My sales work dropped to nothing because I didn't find time for work. They even paid for my car payments to make it easier for me. I thought this was fantastic. Fantastic for me, but not for my family — there was no time for them.

The money floating around gave me a stupendous idea for a business venture. We formed a new insurance company to sell protection to fishermen and hunters. We elected a board of directors and I was to serve as the chairman. The barman was elected president because he put up five grand. The clothier came up with three thousand and he was to be the vice-president with the bodyguard serving as the treasurer. When the funds were depleted from drunken meetings and conferences we were holding every day, new cash flow was added. The insurance company was to sell 25 cent polices for $1000.00 coverage with every fishing or hunting license issued by the state. The corporation papers were all in order and we had a legitimate attorney doing all the legal work for us in Lansing. All of our meetings were held at my house over a bottle and you can guess what kind of planning came out of that.

Typical of heavy drinkers, we were bragging all over the area about the idea we had fostered. Great opportunities do not come around very often. Before we had completed our final authorization, two old line insurance companies grabbed the idea and were in business before we completed our paperwork. We all cried in our soup. All that drunken talent had gone down the drain.

The bodyguard had gone into the hospital for an operation for ulcerated stomach. He accidentally fell out of bed, hit his head on a radiator, and never recovered. He was diagnosed as a victim of acute alcoholism. We gave him a beautiful funeral and went back to the bar and told all his friends that he drank too much. The clothier went back to taking care of his business a little closer because it was getting too hot for him.

The retired barman and I went into some crazy episodes. After drinking solidly for about a week, we went to the local airport and rented out a plane for a couple of hours. For an extra $50.00 bill we had the pilot swoop down over both of our rooftops just for fun. Our next crazy antic a few weeks later was to rent a big speedboat on the Detroit River and to run around dodging other boats. We finally got the driver stiff on liquor we had brought aboard. We then bet him on screwy turns around the steel supports of the Belle Isle and Ambassador Bridges. Why the Lord had saved us I do not know.

After going through about $18,000 worth of drinking, my buddy finally told me about his upcoming trial. He was an accessory to the fact at an incident in his old bar. He would be going away for a while. I also found out why a Pontiac car had followed me constantly for eight months. It was an FBI team of investigators. A close call for me again, but I didn't learn anything from this experience.

Nearing the end of his trial, my retired bar buddy drank very, very heavily. Many times I drove him home. Laying him down on the couch in his living room, he would ask me to turn down the music he thought was coming out of the fireplace — I obliged. There wasn't even a radio in the room. Finally he left for a year and a half and I lost the best drinking buddy a man could ever have. He became sober in prison by joining AA. He has never touched a drink after that. Sadly, it took me another ten years to find sobriety.

There is nothing worse than an alcoholic full of pity who has lost the best job he has ever had in his life. I then decided to visit my ex-Army engineer drinking buddy from the oil family in Pennsylvania. With about $50.00 in my pocket and tank full of gas, I headed for Oil City, Pennsylvania. I was flabbergasted when I found that my old friend had opened up a tobacco shop and had stopped drinking. I couldn't believe it! I still had to cry to him that my wife had thrown me out, the children had no use for me, and no one understood me. What a big lie! I was bitterly disappointed that we couldn't resume our drinking fellowship for a few days. He and his wife were congenial hosts. After spending a restless night at his home without anything to drink, I left the next morning after breakfast.

What a slap in the face for me from an old drinking buddy. I barely made it home without cracking up on the highway. You would think that this incident would open my eyes. Here was a man who was drunk every day of his Army career just like me. He quit drinking the day he arrived home after discharge. This set me back for a few days, but not to quitting like he did.

I shied away from all my newspaper friends. I couldn't stand the thought that they fired such a nice guy who could drink more than they could but didn't have enough sense to stop like they would.

I began looking for new haunts to explore. I found a nice place I thought, because they called it "GI Joes". That became my new second home. The owner was an ex-Marine who had a heart of gold as long as you did not run out of money. This was a gathering place for all kinds of characters including politicians, businessmen, rackateers, and a few high-class bums like me. I kept my image clean here for a long time and had established a good line of credit.

I became friendly with a lot of the owner's relatives. In the years to come, he told me I was one of his "preferred" customers because I spent enough money there for him to buy a new Cadillac every year. What a "nice" reputation. That still didn't bother me because I had an "ego reputation" to keep up and was able to spend more than the other guy. How stupid can you be?

Chapter 11

The Skids

My family had established regular communication with the Olivet Lutheran Church in the neighborhood. Pastor Gruhn kept in close touch with my wife. He also tried to counsel me many times, but I wasn't ready.

The Higher Power that I later found in the church basement must have been a hand on my wife's shoulder. The church and its many activities were the only outlet my family had. I did not even seem to know that they even existed during my sprees. Blackouts and many long periods of time were haphazard. What a selfish attitude the alcohol had created in me. I was in a shell of my own and could not focus the family responsibilities into my own life. I really didn't know why I had to drink so heavily.

It came to a point that I carried my own bottle in the car under the seat. An empty glass would exasperate my patience, even in a bar. We would go to weddings or private parties and I would get angry at the host for being such a slow server. Even a picnic, with all the bottles on a community table, could not satisfy my desire. I thought it looked better to sneak a few from my private bottle in the car. Hiding my habit for lustful drinking became a game with me. Everyone caught on except me, as I slept in the car while they were having a good time.

My dad bought a farm in Brown City, about 40 miles north of Detroit. This was to be his place of retirement. We would go up there every weekend during the summer. The children and my wife enjoyed the country life. This spoiled my lifestyle a bit because I had to somewhat behave myself. My father and mother worked very hard to get the place in shape. My wife did the cooking and the kids usually had a ball. I always found an excuse to go to town to the local hardware store for materials, and thus was able to also make regular stops at the tavern at the Brown City Hotel. I became acquainted with a lot of the patrons and farmers and the town drunks everybody knew. This became useful to me in my future adventures.

The complete remodeling cost approximately three thousand dollars and the place was really modernized. We put in a new well and had running water. My brother came up with all his tools and in one week we had completed a new plumbing and electrical job. My mother had the kitchen cabinets redone and bought a new stove and refrigerator. Working summers and winter weekends, our project was completed in about three years. My father worked hard to fix up the place, but never did live long enough to enjoy this as his retirement home.

Meanwhile, I was drifting around from one sign company to another, never at one place long enough to establish myself. It was easy for me to get along with everyone, but I would quit or I would get out in a short time. Luckily, my progress would lead me to a better position on every move.

Periodic drinking had become my new way of living. For about every three months I would work very hard to get out of debt. Then my ego could not stand the prosperity again. I would jump the track and go on a month's bender. I would be ashamed to go home to sleep. It usually brought me to an all night theater somewhere in downtown Detroit to sleep it off.

On one particular occasion I found myself on Michigan Avenue in the "skid row" area. My bar hopping started in downtown and I made every bar up to Livernois Ave. Having read about the Bowery in New York, I knew what to expect. It was the same: winos on the curb in the mornings ... handouts at the missions ... sleeping at the Salvation Army or at the Trinity Church. At night the bodies would be stacked up in the doorways to keep warm. They would hide their shoes inside their shirts or coats to keep them from getting stolen during the night. What a way to exist!

I lived in this environment for about a week to compare my life with theirs. They were below my dignity, or so I thought. Little did I realize then that I had my own personal "skid row" in the two miles of bars in my neighborhood. This was a real experience for me to meet people of every color and profession. There was a doctor, engineer, architect, teacher, musician, factory workers, and one sign painter. These people were not bums. They just chose to live in that element. Many of them were drifting like I was and were divorced. I was rather disappointed but curious.

Many years later I was to find out that there were over 94 million drinkers out of a 230 million total population. Nine million of these were known alcoholics and ten million were problem drinkers. The funny part, as it is known to most "goodie" drinkers, 5% of the 19 million (950,000) are true skid row bums. Where are the rest of them hiding? Some are women closeted in their kitchens. Many more are like me.

I spent the two days of this reckless adventure on Third Street. This area in downtown Detroit is known as the Cass Corridor and is largely inhabited by open streetwalkers and the destitute. This is one of the bottoms. My interest in women was never strong enough to get involved with any of them. I had a lousy philosophy that would never allow me to pay for a good time. My only ambition on one of these ventures was to get drunk. The last night of my episode I found myself in a sleazy hotel room. Waking up in the moring, I found cigarette burns on my back. Someone must have put a "mickey" in my beer. I don't quite recall. There was a ten dollar bill I had hidden under a doily on the dresser. I took that and went back to the Sweetheart Bar and Jumbo's to drink it up. Here I ran across a bachelor sign painter who was on a thirty day vacation.

We decided to team up for a while. He had no car but he had a lot of brushes and tall ladders. We bought a set of car racks for the top of my car and bought a lot of sign paint to take along. I told him about the farmers I had met in the Brown City Hotel and the silos we could letter around the county. Operating from and staying at the local hotel was good word of mouth advertising for us. The rooms were furnished with antiques, but there were good beds. The only fire escape method was one exit at each end of the hallway. Each room had a steam radiator to which a one-inch rope was attached for escape through the window.

In three weeks we had enough of name lettering on high rise silos and fronts of barns. We sure lived in grand style at the hotel every night. Coming back home, I left some money and took off again to complete my Cass Corridor adventure.

After that I didn't take a drink for about six months. There was no problem until that first drink. Neither my wife nor I could understand why it was impossible for me to stop after once getting started. Alcoholism as a disease was not too acceptable at that time. Besides, I wasn't ready.

My next job came from an Englishman by the name of Sid Chapman. He gave me a position as a designer/salesman. I sold signs during the day and made colored sketches at night. Being busy at what I liked to do best kept me sober. My family started to enjoy their father a little more.

My new employer had a cottage on the Canadian side of the Detroit River. There we spent many good times with the families on weekends. We even started to visit some of our relatives whom we had forsaken. There were a few trips back to Harsen's Island to pick mushrooms. My wife was a great mushroom picker and could smell them a mile away. She knew the good ones and canned quite a few dozen jars.

There was always a drinking urge gnawing in my stomach when times were too good. After that first shot and a beer (my style), it was "off to the races" for me. After a couple of bad relapses, Chapman Signs had to let me go. He couldn't depend on me. The sales were there but the follow-up was vague. I tried the hospital route twice. Another fellow and I had gone to a rehab alcohol hospital on Grand Boulevard and Vernor Highway. Imagine — at that time spending $100.00 a week to have yourself locked up from drinking. At the end of the two week hospital stay, I could hardly wait to get to the nearest bar.

Twice I used this as an excuse to clean up my act but it didn't work. It never does work if you don't have the honesty to admit that the booze has become your master. I took all my problems and put them in a bottle every day. I didn't know how to cope with them. At each day's end, my troubles were at the bottom of an empty bottle. There were also new problems that were picked up each new day. My blackouts came often and it scared me, but not enough to quit drinking. My language was also not too good during these sprees. Never once, my wife tells me, did I ever beat her or the children. Thank God. All the four letter words were bad enough.

Chapter 12

Disastrous Times

Speaking of using abusive words, nothing could fire me up quicker than when Ann called me an alcoholic. Neither one of us knew then or believed that it was a sickness, like diabetes or cancer, and could be controlled by treatment. If she would call me a drunk or a bum it wouldn't have bothered me. Later, with me in AA and her in AL-ANON, we would understand.

I roamed around for a few weeks looking for a new sign company to hire me. One look at my condition, however, was enough for most potential employers to turn me down. I had one special bar where I had done some work and sold the owner a new display for his rooftop. He owed me about $2200.00. I had set him up on a monthly payment plan of $200.00. My drinking got heavier and I was always using the payments in advance. He was a veteran and we had many common interests. He trusted me explicitly. Every day that I would come in he would set me up my favorite bottle in front of me and leave it there. From the very beginning he knew that I couldn't stand an empty glass. As long as it was full I was alright. I could gulp it down and pour another. If you know what it did to an alcoholic's ego. I was the only patron allowed that privilege. Wow! Was I a big shot - supposedly. Then he would come over, pick up my twenty dollar bill and say, how many did you have? That really made me feel important and trustworthy. When I was short he would extend me a bar tab - another downfall to an alchy. Many times my next sign payment was used up in advance this way.

Towards the latter part of my heavy drinking at his place, he told me, as a friend, to cut down. He said, "If you keep up at that rate you're going, you will die. I will see that you get a nice funeral." That didn't scare me. Little did I know that he later became a heavy drinker himself. About 15 years hence he died in the basement of a church rehab center. We gave him a beautiful military ceremony.

My mother was living on the family farm then full time while my father worked in the city and only went up on weekends. He was very good to our children, especially to my son Ted. Ted would follow my father like a little puppy. Everything he ever learned about tools and carpentry rubbed off on him from watching my father. My son was in closer communication with my folks than I was. My father felt very sorry for my wife and was constantly giving her financial assistance. He would shake his head back and forth and say "Ted, Ted, when are you going to wake up?"

The children were getting big enough to appreciate the farm life, staying there all summer long. The forty acres of farm land were leased out on a co-op basis. The livestock consisted of a milking cow, two nanny goats, some rabbits, and about fifty chickens. My little boy sat for hours amusing himself watching the chickens scratching and eating. He always had a willow switch handy to hit the rooster when he jumped the chickens. He thought the rooster would kill the hens. Later we explained.

After a while, my father began to show some signs of illness. He wouldn't go to a doctor. My drinking had become so bad it made him very irritable and he told me to move. We found a nice place in Dearborn with reasonable rent. At this point there was an ad for a real estate salesman in the local paper. Applying for the position, I was hired and passed the exam for my license on my first attempt. During my high school days I used to hang around a real estate and insurance office for about six months and learned some of the ramifications. I never forgot the background experience. The realtor soon found out my "secret" drinking style. I had to leave, but I continued to renew my license every year.

My wife and I went to a couple of open AA meetings and I attended several closed ones. What a bunch of panty-waists! I thought they quit drinking because they couldn't afford it. I was just looking for stupid excuses not to give this wonderful AA program a chance. I paid the long price and kept on drinking.

By then I had received my third drunk driving ticket. Having no money this time for an attorney, I was sentenced by the judge to serve ten days. At that time DeHoco (Detroit House of Corrections) was a place where you could either go to AA or buy a bottle. For the record, I went to one AA meeting and didn't learn a thing. How much more beating must it take to open my eyes???

All this was happening during the Christmas holidays. My family had no money, no food, no gifts, and their father was in jail. Hard to believe! The landlady told my wife about the Goodfellows. The Goodfellows saved the holidays for my family. I have been forever grateful to that bunch of guys. After getting out of the pokey, my brother had heard about my situation and offered me a job.

My brother had obtained a blanket contract for the construction of a new facility for electro-plating auto parts. The job didn't pay much, but drinking could be very easily hidden in the plant. With my brother being the superintendent, it was easy for me. Being on the night shift was even better. He would assign me certain tasks and I would work at my leisure. Having the key to the front door made it convenient for me to come and go as I pleased. There was a bar about 300 feet away from the plant. After many visits and closing the bar at 2:30 a.m., I would lay down to sleep a while. I night latched the lock so everyone had to ring a bell to get in, even if they had a key. I had a few unexpected visitors, but was never caught drinking. For security reasons, they let me keep the place on night lock. After a little snooze I would work extra hard to catch up.

This kept going on during almost ten months of construction. Even today it is impossible to believe the physical abuse that my body had endured. My brother had a great capacity for alcohol, but he showed up for work every day. I was a periodic and this was my longest stretch of daily drinking.

My brother would visit us and tell my folks that I drank too much. They believed him. He always left all kinds of AA literature behind for me to read. God rest his soul today. Eventually that reading moved me to a steady diet of AA when I finally surrendered and admitted that Lord Calvert was my master. But it took a little more time.

My father's health was on a downhill grade after they discovered he had cancer of the stomach. When they opened him up the second time to cut out some more, it had spread to his liver. It was too late to do any more for him. He died in about eight weeks. Instead of being near my mother during these critical times, they found me in the back seat of my dad's car — stone drunk. My conscience still bothers me today, after more than twenty years of sobriety, that I had been such a miserable son.

After my father's death, we moved back to live with my mother because of her loneliness. I behaved for quite some time, but the urge came back. She wanted her house painted inside and out. She furnished the materials and the labor would be paid in cash. I immediately took an advance and was always running out of turpentine so I could go to the nearest bar. My favorite place was known as "GI Joe's". He understood my problem, knowing me from way back. My credit was always good there to carry me over. The painting job took about seven weeks to complete and I bought a lot of turpentine. I recall that by the time the job was done my mother did not owe me a dime. It was a good thing she gave a lot of the money for the job to my wife.

Many times my wife would hide my car keys. I would rebel and be gone for a couple of days. This prompted me to get duplicate sets made and hide them. There was an emergency set wired under the seat. What emergency? Many times my clothes were hidden to keep me from going out. That's quite a challenge for an alcoholic. I told my wife if she didn't give me back my clothes, I would leave in my PJs. I tied a scarf around my neck with a stick pin for decoration. I used a pair of high rubber boots to cuff in my pajamas. A beret, car coat, and a fancy cane transformed me into a Frenchman upon reaching the bar.

How crazy can you get? Another time my wife had again hidden all my clothes. Nonchalantly, I walked around the house picking up all kinds of apparel to wear. I found enough to wear except for shoes. Would you believe — I walked out on a bitter cold night in very thin rubber overshoes. A couple of hours later, the door of GI Joe's opened and my shoes were thrown in by my children.

I had become a drunken bum in my own neighborhood. The death of a salesman had arrived. It wasn't necessary to go on Michigan Avenue or Third Street any more. I had my own skid row. My sprees got more frequent and my mother sold the house. She couldn't stand the memories of my father in that home and I was of no help. She went to live with my sister.

Laying off the booze for a while, I landed a job in Mt. Clemens as a sign salesman. It was strictly a commission job and I did rather well. My first landlady was a salesperson at a real estate office. I started to figure if I kept busy enough that drinking would go away. Later I was to find out in AA that keeping busy was one of the key formulas to sobriety. I sold signs during the day and worked part time in the real estate office during the night. There were many Polish clients who did business at this real estate office. My knowledge of the Polish language surfaced to a useful purpose and we prospered for a while.

My mother was looking to buy another house. I told her to be patient and I would use my commission to help her. She was interested in an income place and wanted us again to move in with her. It was nice to do something for her for a change. Finding a clean piece of property about five blocks from the realtor, we were together again.

The new adventure into real estate took a misdirection. There were too many twenty dollar bills in my pocket. Such prosperity burned a hole in my pocket, and I took off on another spree. My memory was going bad on me. Many times I walked around my car looking for tell-tale marks the next morning. I couldn't remember where I had been or what I had done. It was insanity showing up.

Chapter 13

Insane Living

As they say around AA, it takes one to know one. One day I ran across a sign painter in my neighborhood who opened up a shop and liked to drink as much as I did. We became great friends over night. I continuously hung around helping him turn out some work. All he made was spent on drinks and here I became what you call a pro wino. A bottle of wine was cheap, and you could stay high all day just sipping. Drinking a glass of water the next morning would put you where you left off the night before. He had a cot in back and slept there many nights because he was too drunk to go home. His mother lived in a housing project and many a cold night I slept there in a chair or on the floor. What a way to go down and down on my skid row.

One particular morning after closing a bar, I was driving home and went through a red light at an intersection about a half mile from my house. I hit a Bible salesman's car broadside. I staggered out of my car and helped him pick up his bibles that had scattered everywhere. Again the hand of God was on my shoulder. As a Christian man, he understood my problem. We exchanged addresses and I left my car there in the traffic lane until the following morning. I went to pick it up and there wasn't even a ticket on the windshield. I had it towed to a garage for extensive repairs. The Bible salesman had to have two plastic surgery operations on his face. I never received a bill from him for hospital treatment or for the repairs to his car. He could have sued me for life. I certainly was grateful for that one!

I had to celebrate my good luck with another drink. But from then on, I promised myself never to drive when I drank too much. So I did a lot of sleeping in the back seat of my car using my briefcase as a pillow. My favorite last bar before going home was about three blocks from my house. I could easily sleep behind the bar or stagger home through the alley. Many times I would get up and didn't remember how I got home or where the car was parked. Sometimes I spent hours going from one bar to the next not remembering where I was last. On one occasion, I was walking across the street to my last bar and was hit and thrown in the air about twenty feet without any serious injury except a few minor scratches. The driver gave me a ten dollar bill and I recrossed the street to the same bar and got loaded.

In the bar I met a couple going to a party and I tagged along. The people I met there were very congenial and told me to have a good time. They told me not to worry if I drank too much because I could go to sleep on their couch, which I later did. In the morning we were awakened by a knock on the front door. My wife boldly walked in and proceeded to make a catastrophe out of the living room. She tore down the drapes, swept a typewriter off a table, and literally left the place in a shambles. She did hundreds of dollars worth of damage and I thought I was in real trouble there. She didn't want to believe that I only slept on the couch. It was all forgotten when I went out and bought another bottle.

Another time a couple of guys dropped me off in front of the house. I tried to climb the three steps onto my front porch. I never made it and fell into the shrubbery. I must have layed there quite a while and it was cold outside. My next door neighbor lady saw me and came over and helped me out of my dilemma. She rang my door bell and ran. I fell when I got in the house and hit my forehead on a door hinge resulting in a very bad wound. I refused to go to a hospital for stitches and even tore off a bandaid my wife had put on to close the cut. How much more could she put up with? It didn't bother me one bit because an alcoholic is a very selfish and ungrateful person.

One of my favorite things to do to new bartenders was to fool them for an hour with crazy antics. I always carried extra clothes on these occasions. Walking into certain bars, I would amble to the center section and order a drink. After a few minutes of conversation with the bartender and surrounding patrons and after belting down a few, I would leave by the back door with some change remaining at the bar.

My car was parked at the rear and I would put on a bow tie, a different hat and a different jacket. Coming back through the front door, I would go all the way to the end of the bar in the rear. Changing brands and altering my voice, I would start a different conversation on another topic. After a few minutes I would ask the bartender to bring my change from the middle of the bar.

"Sorry, that's not yours," he said. The guy is in the restroom. I would go to the restroom, come out, and tell him that no one was in there. Naturally he checked, and was really baffled and didn't know who was going nuts. This provoked a full blast argument. Finally going out and coming back in the original clothes kept me from being thrown out.

To top this scenario, I would go back out to the car, put on a turban and dark glasses, and use a large scarf for a veil. Coming back in, I would park myself in the last booth next to the restrooms. I lit a candle, put it in an ashtray, pulled out a small fortune-telling ball on which to meditate. Ordering a double drink with a foreign accent, I asked the bartender not to bother me until I called him.

Curiosity killed a cat, and those going to relieve their holding tanks would pause momentarily. Upon returning, they would sit down and ask me to read their fortunes. Looking like a real swami, I had a ball and the drinks were flying free.

One time my favorite bar owner was celebrating his

twentieth anniversary and he naturally invited his best customers. This is the one who said I spent enough to buy him a Cadillac every year. As usual, I had to get loaded before we got there. Upon arriving, we had one drink, nothing to eat, and insisted upon leaving immediately. Driving away in the wrong direction down Davison Avenue, my car was weaving and ended up in the police station parking lot. I was going to go in and get the right directions to get me home. I wouldn't listen to my wife. Again, the only Buddy I had up above kept me out of jail. I sobered up in a big hurry when I read the sign "Davison Police Station".

Crazy, crazy, insane living!!! The only thing that really mattered to me was my next bottle.

Chapter 14

Bottom Out

My drinking escapades now became one continuous drunk; I stopped being a periodic. I could not control myself anymore. Then a bright idea came to me one morning. I would try to be a social drinker for a change. Mayor LaGuardia of New York had a nice style of drinking, and I liked class. He would never take a drink until 5:00 p.m. I tried it for four days and it almost killed me. It still didn't register in my mind that my life had become unmanageable and that I was powerless over alcohol. After that very short period of social drinking and closing up the bar at 2:30 a.m., I went back to my regular diet of getting drunk three times a day. My consumption had

increased to over two fifths a day with a bottle beside
my bed when I finally tried to go to sleep.

Promises, promises ... nothing was new. How
many times I told myself, "Ted, this is it. How much
can you hate yourself to keep on doing this? How
about your family?" I would talk to myself endlessly.
Was I going insane? When I lay down on the back seat
of my car, or on my own bed when possible, the
picture wasn't pleasant. The fantasy of high living
had turned to shakes and tremors. I would sweat for a
while until a swig of the bottle would quiet me down.

One day I was rummaging in the basement looking
for old bottles to cash in when I discovered that the
cool-room was padlocked. A challenge! The alcoholic
mind went to work right away. There must be
something in there that must be important. However,
the trick was to get in without a key or without
showing forced entry. Taking the door off the hinges,
I discovered a crock of fermenting wine. Wow! What
a goldmine, and right in my own basement! An alkies
fantasy dream had finally come true.

In a round-about conversation with my mother and
my wife, I found out that it was raspberry wine. They
had picked the berries in our backyard. It was to be
mature by Christmas. Well, be assured, this twenty
gallon festivity never made it to the holidays. The
crock was my daily stopover between bar-hopping. I
never gave the mash a chance to do its job. Imagine
drinking raw wine for two months. What a
disappointment to my mother. Her son proved to be a
real "crockie". To try to make some kind of
restitution, I brought home a big bottle of

champagne. I offered it to my mother and asked for forgiveness. She did forgive me after some tears. We hurt the ones closest to us without even giving it a second thought.

As a "periodic drunk" I was always making pledges to stop drinking. These pledges only lasted a short time. Thousands of times I told my wife, "Honey, I'll never take another drink as long as I live." She stopped believing me a long time ago. I couldn't fool her too often. It's funny how they get to know the symptoms. Many times I would sweat it out for three days, shave off a week's growth of whiskers, borrow a fiver from her for a haircut, dress up like a successful salesman, and away I went. She never knew whether this was it or not. Usually when I said I wasn't going to have a drink I meant it but somehow or other I eventually took that drink. The first one was the one that got me in trouble every time, but my ego wouldn't let me believe that. There was always another excuse.

I must tell you that up until now the hangovers never bothered me. Of course, the first three drinks that I took at 6:00 a.m. after opening a bar were managed with two hands. Oh brother, now I could manage the rest of the day, bumming. I was broke so many times and envied the man who came into the bar, pulled out a roll of dough, and bought the crowd a few rounds of drinks. He was a big shot to me — just like I used to be. He had money with which to buy drinks. The day before that it was me — now I was sick, ashamed, thirsty, and broke.

It's funny, but it takes one to know one and he

would quickly send me a couple of shots and a beer. Being a good conversationalist, we would spend the whole morning talking. The next day I couldn't even remember his name. Blackouts were coming closer together and sometimes I couldn't put the last three days together. I became an expert at getting drunk without a dime in my pocket. Me, a big wheel, finally hit the bottom. I had become a "skid" in my own neighborhood. And I thought the bums on Michigan Avenue, Third Street, or the Cass Corridor were bad! But I didn't let it bother me.

My binges were getting shorter and shorter because I was running out of money, friends to get a loan from, and bars that would extend me credit. The local police knew me well and stopped taking me home. They warned me that if I kept on sleeping on the back seat of my car, they would lock me up. So I moved to a new environment until everyone caught on. Detroit is a big city, but I was getting hemmed in. The roof was falling in, but I still held on — one drink at a time.

I still had a few bucks in the bank so the account could stay open. I overdrew my balance and received a letter stating that my account had been closed. I knew the manager from the good old days of business and prosperity and wrote him back. Nothing happened. So I wrote to him again. The manager responded by calling my house with an ultimatum.

Conditions at home were going from bad to worse. There were arguments all the time. My speech was full of abusive words. I came home from an escapade one afternoon and discovered that my son Ted, 17 at the time, had left home. He had packed up his clothes and a few belongings to go to my daughter Gloria's house. He still had one year of high school left before graduation. I had a boisterous discussion with my wife over that but it was to no avail. That same night my wife had already made arrangements with my other daughter Patricia to move out. When I came home my wife was already gone.

They couldn't do this to a nice guy like me — a father who provided so generously for his family. My ego was shattered completely for the first time in my life. They bruised my pride. Why should I worry that they left me flat? Here was a 47-year-old drunk with a mother who still would take care of him. In pity my mother loaned me a twenty dollar bill and away I went to the nearest bar. Neither one of us wanted to believe that I was a very sick man and that I had the disease of alcoholism. We only wanted to believe that I drank too much and didn't stop until I passed out.

Chapter 15

Candle on the Table

After a binge that went on for four days, I got up the next morning with my doorbell ringing. With my system full of wine for the last few days, I was spinning around when I answered the door. My son-in-law stood there like a giant from space. He was 6'3" and he scared me that morning. I wasn't too nice to him, especially when I found out that he came for the rest of my wife's clothes. He just stood there outside waiting. I gathered as much as I could and threw them at him. What a way to treat a good guy who was only trying to do right under the circumstances.

I had a bottle of wine left and I spent the rest of the day brooding and sipping, crying to myself. I was blaming everybody for my situation except big wheel me. I started looking for some loose money in all the drawers or something valuable to pawn like I had tried to do once with our expensive silverware set before Ann caught me at the door. I had forgotten that she had taken her valuables to our daughter's place. I still had an expensive 1823 genuine Geunerius violin that I figured would bring me a nice sum for the next day at a downtown auction house. Then something happened to me.

After a thorough search, I found only thirteen cents and a bunch of AA material. My brother had brought this for me to read about ten years ago. Today I can say that it was the Higher Power who directed me to that particular drawer. I stopped dead in my tracks and started reading the pamphlets for three solid hours. Bleary-eyed, I finally layed down to rest my eyes and had a good snooze for the first time in years. Getting up with a little peace of mind, I remembered that there was an AA meeting that night in the basement of my church.

I drove around the block three times before I parked in the church lot. Coming through the door, I noticed the Candle on the table. I slunk into a chair like the whipped dog I was. At first I thought I was sitting with a new type of religious sect. The fuse had burned out in the basement - hence the candle. That was the light that opened my eyes for once. They invited me to the "first step" table and I felt a little better because there were a few other first timers like me. I listened and found out that I wasn't alone in all my troubles. They were there for help too. I desperately needed someone's help. What did I have to lose — they told me I could go back to my drinking any time. They wouldn't tell me what to do.

AA told me not to compare myself to others and I didn't. It was my third exposure to AA and I decided to give it a fair shake. Imagine, me, giving the AA a break! I had spent 32 years of resentment, egotism, and dishonesty in character. I was going to really listen and try to practice the program this time around.

The first step was a real stopper for me. They told me that if I admitted to being powerless over alcohol and admitted that my life had become unmanageable, I had it half licked. Well, that seemed pretty easy, but would I be honest with myself? Could I admit that I was a failure at drinking? I could drink like a gentleman!

Fifty percent recovery upon admittance sounded like a good deal. I couldn't con these guys — they were all pros. In back of my mind the wheels were spinning the tune "You never have any trouble until you take that first drink — why take it?" Taking it made my life go out of kilter. I threw a lot of questions at them and got some very sensible answers.

The AA meeting ended and I was just about ready to leave when a fellow by the name of Mike K., a milkman with his own route, came up to me. He asked if I would like to go to the Alano Club where they have discussions until after midnight. I reminded Mike that he had to get up for work about 3:00 a.m. He said not to worry. It was at that meeting that I found out that these fellows would do anything at any hour to help you achieve and maintain sobriety. It was difficult for a selfish man like me to understand.

I was introduced to a nice gent named Frank C. and I was blessed with two sponsors in one night. After 2:00 a.m. Frank said he would pick me up for a meeting at eight in the morning, Well, my evening of drinking was spoiled by two meetings and this guy was picking me up so early. I could not understand these people. They were sitting around talking about their drinking, their personal problems, and they were happy. They were laughing and joking. They all had smiles on their faces. At first I thought they were a bunch of yo-yo's. But soon I was to learn the difference. They could have fun drinking coffee and didn't need booze any more.

I immediately took a liking to this bunch of ex's and continued to attend meetings every night at different locations. I stopped crying about all the drinking buddies I lost. Here were hundreds of new friends and I didn't need any money to be with them. Oh, they passed the basket at the end of the night, but you didn't have to contribute. Also — I was very impressed because they were self supporting.

After about two weeks, this way of life fascinated me. I went back to one of my old sign company owners and resold myself on a trial basis. It was only on commission but it was a new start. Well, I was making graphic sketches, sometimes with both hands, but that was my pattern all my life. Play hard - drink hard - work hard.

With a few deals closed, I was able to pay some old

bills, get my car out of back payments, and get out of debt with my mother. I called my wife and told her about my new attitudes. I was looking at everything from a positive angle — no more negativism. She wanted to believe me but didn't. She even turned down the money I offered her. That really hurt my ego.

I had learned in that short time not to let things like that throw you. I even attended a Sunday service in my church upstairs. They were really happy to see me after a three year absence. It's a good thing the family kept going regularly and had spiritual communication. I was to obtain mine later. After about a month of nervous sobriety and trying to swallow the twelve steps of AA, my wife decided to come home and to give me a chance under the AA umbrella.

Chapter 16

Soul Searching

I ran too fast with all those sobriety steps and almost choked. AA taught me to take one step at a time until I could handle another one. It was easier that way. When I took up the second step, I came to believe that a Power greater than ourselves could restore us to sanity. The third step asked us to make a decision to turn our wills and our lives over to the care of God as we understand Him. I didn't think too much about it because I was going to church regularly and that would take care of those steps.

When I started to do some real soul searching, I saw a different meaning. I couldn't stop drinking once I started the first one. Already a Power greater than myself had helped me the past thirty days, so I left it at that. Still a little skeptical about my own faith as I had been taught, I did turn it over to that Power without question. It was easier for me to have Him handle my spiritual connection. It was always my belief to have experts handle their own thing. After all, who am I to doubt an expert! I turned over the entire situation to Him and that made the entire situation easier for me to handle. I was not in a position right then to dig any deeper on that subject.

It worked for me pretty well for a beginner. Of course I received some fantastic help from the Serenity Prayer:

> *God grant me the serenity to accept the things*
> *I cannot change ... the courage to change the*
> *things I can ... and the wisdom to know the*
> *difference.*

This prayer is used as an opener for every AA meeting. it sure helped me in many, many situations, but especially in not taking that first drink. Even to this day it is one of the strongest tools of my continued sobriety.

I knew that this new lifestyle was not my brand. My will and life had to be turned over to His care because my pattern had been rotten all these years. Don't think that all at once I became a "Holy Joe" or a reformer. No siree! It's just that I could manage this style of living just a little bit better. Many people were helping me in the same way that they had been helped. I couldn't do it alone — I had already proven that. Besides, no one was telling me what I had to do. I was

doing it on my own with the Higher Power I had
discovered by accident. I knew that I had only two
choices. One choice was to take that first drink and
get back on the merry-go-round trying to catch that
golden ring. My second choice was to stay with this
beautiful new-found fellowship in AA.

Being inquisitive about my new association, I
discovered there were over 20,000 groups in the USA
and that I was one of 600,000 members. I never felt so
big in my life. The stigma of an alcoholic was not
bothering me very much — I was not alone. Besides,
Lord Calvert was not my master any more. He didn't
have a ring in my nose — the yoke was off my back. I
WAS FREE — as long as I didn't take that first drink.
But that I didn't need it did not mean I didn't crave it
any longer.

Pride had turned to self-esteem, anger to tolerance.
I lived only one day at a time — it was easier that way.
I was elated with my new successes. I was making
money. My wife was showing a little more happiness
around the house. She had proven herself a real
Florence Nightingale. Many times she had nursed me
back to health on the verge of total collapse. Now I
was able to show a little gratitude.

By going to open meetings together, Ann found
out about Al-Anon, the special group of wives and
husbands of alcoholics who share together their
problems of coping with their mates. God bless them!
After a period of sobriety it is hard for the non-
alcoholic to live with a sober ex-drunk. Believe me,
it's a different world. They also have to admit and
accept. Ann's attendance in this group greatly helped

my sobriety. We had many of the same old problems without the drinking, but it was much easier to deal with them.

I skipped around on AA's steps to sobriety and used what I thought was important to me and my family. I also took a searching and fearless moral inventory of myself. New priorities were set up and I made a list of all my defects and tried hard to work on them. I was doing so well it scared me. We were sometimes going to meetings seven days or nights a week. I found time to visit a hospital and a jailhouse. I was really getting involved.

Everything was going along beautifully for eleven months and twenty days. At the next regular monthly AA meeting, I was to get my one year AA pin with a birthday cake. Unexpectedly, my brother and his wife had come up from Texas to visit. I played the host by going out and getting a case of beer and a bottle of whiskey. Well, after three hours of talking and coaxing to have only one for old times sake, old barley corn took over and you know what happened. Just that one drink did it. We drank together for two solid days.

The third morning I stepped out on the back porch for some fresh air in my shorts and leaned too hard on the banister. It gave way and I fell about fifteen feet and landed on a shrub. I missed the back stairs by six inches. Now you can call it what you want, but again my Higher Power had saved me for something. The first time I was saved was on Harsen's Island by not running into the river. The other times included getting hit by a car and being thrown twenty feet into the air, hitting a bible salesman broadside, and now falling from the second floor.

Naturally my brother offered to take me to the hospital. We got as far as the nearest bar. I didn't want my wife to go along because the "stinkin-thinkin-drinkin" took over. Well, we drank for about two hours and came home. I told them at home that everything was all right and that we had just dropped in the bar for a short time. I was right back where I was eleven months ago — in the ditch. I never made it to the hospital that day. The next day I was in severe pain and my wife and I went to the hospital on this trip. A fractured rib is all that I suffered on that fall.

My brother and his wife left for Texas and I went right back to my wino pattern and the bottom. I was sitting and sipping under the apple tree in my backyard when I got the feeling someone else was there — but I was alone! My brain heard someone telling me, "Buddy, you may never sober up this fourth time around." LET GO AND LET GOD ... and I dumped the rest of the bottles behind the garage.

That night I ran to the AA meeting at a school a few blocks from home. Was I glad to get back! I told them to forget about the anniversary cake and pin. All they said was to remember "easy does it and do it one day at a time" and the new year will run for you. I absolutely shook from that close call to oblivion. I finally realized that alcoholism is a disease showing no mercy. I also learned again that it was controllable — don't take that first drink.

Chapter 17

New Dedication— AMVETS

I went faithfully to AA meetings with the burning desire to learn. One of the greatest lessons was to keep busy all the time. It was important to be involved in doing different things than were done in the past. I switched employment to one of the largest custom sign manufacturers in the area. The owner knew about my past drinking habits but was willing to go along — another big boost for me.

Establishing contact with the biggest restaurant supply house, I soon had about seventy percent of the finest eating and cocktail places as my clients. This led to further contacts in the Auto Dealer Association and also some theater chains. This new year of happy sobriety flew by quickly and we were celebrating my first AA anniversary in March 1963. I still carry that AA coin. Sometimes I can't find it for months. It shows up in the oddest places to tell everyone what I am. It's my calling card many times — I'm so proud.

Soon after, I attended the funeral of a veteran who was a friend of mine and again my Higher Power showed me a new direction. Our sheet metal man at our plant was trying for months to get me to join his organization, a veterans' group called AMVETS. One of the main reasons for joining at this time was their moving military observance for their deceased members. At that time I never dreamt that this group would lead me to my "top".

In the meantime, my involvement in the church was getting heavier. They showed me great respect by appointing me to an unexpired council seat. In three months the entire congregation elected me for a three year term to the church council. I was really excited, and in my acceptance speech I thanked them for choosing an ex-drunk to be on the council. After all, they knew then and now.

After six months in the AMVETS, I learned my first lesson in politics. There was a special interest group within our post that was wheeling and dealing and the membership was unhappy except for a few. It was nearing election time and one "independent" was running for post commander. They approached me to run against him. I knew nothing about the internal politics but they told me not to worry. After the votes were cast on election night, I won by six votes. My opponent and I became the best of friends. He already knew about my drinking problem and respected the AA for their help to a relative of his. He became my right hand, advisor, and personal "guard" against some smarty spiking my orange juice — a few times they tried to. My AA meetings were top priority. The two sponsors began to worry about my sudden and great interest in AMVETS. It was an old saying around the tables that to stay sober you must change your environment from the drinking element completely. Veterans always had a reputation for two fisted drinking — the best bunch of elbow benders in the country. But I found a new purpose and dedication — giving of myself in time and money, extensive weekly hospital work, and using my creative ability to develop new programs within the community.

I was the busiest guy around. I also saw a fertile field of potential candidates for the AA program. Statistics proved that ten percent of all veterans have a drinking problem. There were over twenty million veterans on record. I felt very safe, always praying for guidance from my Supreme Commander as I now called Him. Every day I openly talked to Him, asking Him to hold me by the hand. My complete reliance on Him made me stronger every day. It has worked for me fabulously — but it may not be the answer for you.

The achievement of getting a new "baby" in AA was an added thrill. He was a concession manager for a large theater chain. Going over to this man's house one day, we talked over his driveway fence for two hours. Something compatible was reached in that first encounter. He made it to his first AA meeting that night. One year later he earned his AA pin and is still sober today.

The twelfth AA step proved to me that I could carry the message. He is a good "paper member" of the AMVETS post and participates in most fundraisers. My two sponsors, Mike K. and Frank C., and the "new baby" Walter O., attended every rally, conference, and convention in many states as well as in Canada. You might ask how we found the time for all of this. Simple — we used the same 24 hour periods for better things. I once worried what I would do without my drinking friends. Would you believe — not one of them ever called me or my wife to ask how we were doing. And I called them friends? No, they were only friends when you bought them drinks.

Our AMVETS post was strongly involved in the needs of the local community. With a large committee, we started a "Shoeless American" program to gather surplus children's shoes, etc. and shipped trailer after trailer to destitute areas in the South. We made a drop-off box at the nearest bank for collection and received much publicity.

We saw the need locally for a Memorial Day Parade. This was a wonderful Americanism program involving all the local schools, churches, boy scout and girl scout troops, the ROTC, homeowner and business groups, police and fire departments, bands, etc. It is an hour long parade with five divisions with many local children participation. At that time this was the only all AMVET parade, sponsored by the Outer-Van Dyke AMVETS Post 27, in the country. It is still going strong after existing over twenty years.

It was also a great instrument for the revival of patriotism in the neighborhood.

One of the greatest programs put together by my post committee was Operation Safety. It was a traffic safety package geared to local high school students. The program attracted national attention and I was called in to the AMVETS national headquarters in Washington, D.C. Over a three day weekend at the executive director's home, this program was updated, changed to a national scope, and "Operation DE" (Driver Excellence) was born. The Dodge Division of the Chrysler Corporation became our partner in safety as a sponsor. This program still continues today and it now involves over 25,000 high schools and a quarter million students in over 40 states. The aim and purpose of the DE Program is to make driver training students more aware of the importance of safer driving on the streets and highways. The program consists of local, state, and national competitions among the best drivers in the country. Four facets are used to select the very best: the skill course, written test, evasive manuever, and the panic stop. Thousands of dollars in scholarships are awarded to the top seven students who reach the national level. It is the only traffic safety program in high schools sanctioned by the National Association of Secondary School Principals. When I was ready to move up politically in AMVETS, all this national exposure I received certainly didn't hurt. Don't forget that all this work was strictly done on a volunteer basis. No one was given any renumeration above legitimate expenses.

It is funny how animals have more common sense than people at times. My daughter Gloria had a dog named Coco. I had never abused him, but when I was drinking he shied away from me. Now after three years of dryness, everybody around me had more or less forgiven me. One day Gloria came over with this poodle and he jumped on my lap as I sat on the couch. He reached up and kissed my ear. I hollered in glee to my wife. Look, even Coco has recognized my sobriety. We had it made thereafter.

Chapter 18

Joys of Sobriety

Just about this time I had a little setback. My one AA sponsor Mike K. was killed in a robbery attempt on his milk route. My activities had decreased somewhat because of my heavy veterans agenda. I had made dozens of AA talks around the various groups and at a few regional gatherings. My compulsion in this new direction was even greater than in the drinking sprees. I was not a "periodic" in this new lifestyle.

The lessons of AA had taught me to foresee all the pitfalls and handle myself with optimism at every step. I had made many amends to those closest to me and paid back thousands of dollars in debts and bar bills. The last one took ten years. My goals for advancement were being achieved one at a time.

I moved through AMVETS offices at the post and at the district levels. At the same time I filled a vacancy as a delegate to the Allied Veterans Council. The council is an organization of nearly twenty top veterans groups and was located in downtown Detroit and encompassed entire Wayne County. In 1966 I received the AMVET of the Year Award for Wayne County. This was the biggie, and I was honored the following year at the Michigan State Fair as their Veteran of the Year.

You may ask yourself how I was able to handle all these awards, accolades, banquets, etc. without the ego breaking out. Well, it was rather easy following the AA principles and traditions. I knew it was good for everybody but Ted to take a drink. There were so many good things happening that I never once failed to indulge in the secret formula — keep busy, busy, busy.

The church council elected me as their president, a position I held for three years. The Mayor of the City of Warren appointed me to the City Beautification Commission to draw up a master plan for parks. I didn't get to make a fortune financially. However, I felt more secure in my sobriety because I was afraid my ego might not stand the prosperity. I couldn't stand it during my binges. Two fifty dollar bills in my pocket and I was a goner. But now I was dry and belonged to the exclusive club of happy sobriety. I was not buying new Cadillacs for bar owners every year. I didn't need as much money — money was only secondary. I worked on my "needs" and the "wants" came as a bonus.

It was rather difficult to keep my anonymity because by this time many people knew that I didn't drink and that AA kept me sober. I didn't try to hide it and was able to move many people in the right direction when they asked for help. Patience, honesty, and humility kept me on the right track. The public relations people were very helpful with the right kind of publicity. I do, however, respect everyone else's anonymity and always will.

My public image now rated A-1. I had no resentments. I was more honest with myself and with others. I had grown spiritually and emotionally with both groups of my new found friends. What a great world! There was a different kind of happiness around the house. My mother could hardly believe the turn around. AA gave me serenity of purpose and the opportunity to be of service to my Supreme Commander above and to the people around me. You receive peace of mind in the exact same proportion as the peace of mind you bring into the lives of people around you. It works in funny ways. At first I actually thought that AA would teach me how to handle sobriety.

I went through the AMVETS offices on the state level. While being Junior Vice Commander, I had developed a vehicle for future membership rallies in a film called "The AMVET Story". It was very helpful to me as membership director the following year. We had set a goal of 1001 members in 1971 and reached that goal in fifteen months. The ultimate office of

State Commander was attained in 1972. That was a fantastic year of state-wide travel of over 30,000 miles. Going out of office, I ran for National Executive Committeeman and lost by six votes. I learned once more that in politics all the credentials and accomplishments in the world won't help you if you haven't got the vote count on the morning of the election. There is victory in defeat if you've learned something. I did - I lost the election after I went to bed at 3:30 that morning.

But with the bad news came some good news the following week. In all the dozens of jobs that I had held in the past, I never left in bad taste or with resentment. I was now working part-time at a real estate office and doing well. The time schedule was very flexible and it nicely suited my extra-curricular activities. People were very good to me that way, knowing my community involvements. A call came from my last big time sign company asking if I would be interested in making $200.00 or more a day.

I went for an interview the next morning. The first thing I asked my prospective boss was if this was such a great job, why give it to me? He explained that it would be a travelling job and I would exclusively cover five states. This new challenge sounded good but it would mean being away from home for short periods. Exposure to strange places, restaurants, cocktail dining rooms in hotels, etc., would be new to me. My wife had no doubt about my slipping back to drinking.

I accepted the offer and formed a new company called Ted Lesk Associates. I became a consultant to the sign industry and serviced the largest automobile manufacturer with their corporate identity sign program. A title like that alone deserved a lot of money and I was another notch on the way to success. In my briefcase I had a USA directory of AA groups. Every time my fellowship tank was getting low, I would stop in to fill up whether I was in Chicago, Pittsburgh, New York, Trenton, Xenia, or elsewhere. There were AA groups anyplace I stayed overnight.

Again the Higher Power had moved me towards my new goal: to be the AMVETS National Commander in six years. My travel on the job enabled me to visit many AMVET posts within my circle and still maintain my association with AA groups. There was no loneliness on these trips. This new sweetheart contract enabled me to be in contact with auto dealers, zone and district managers, and city officials all over my territory. What a job for an alcoholic, I thought for a moment. Free drinks at lunch and at dinner and they would pick up the tab. The old me would have never made it to the next city the following morning.

While in high school over thirty years ago, I had taken six weeks of drafting. Now I was able to put it to good use. The surveys consisted of a plot plan of the dealership facility and elevation drawing of their showroom and service building. Right and left photographs of the showroom and I was in business. Knowing how to read blueprints saved a thousand steps. Checking with the zoning and sign ordinance of each community and making recommendations as to placement of the assigned package of dealership signs was all there was to it.

Each survey paid a flat fee and I could easily do two or three a day. After a week to ten days on the road, I would work in my home office for about two weeks. I would complete the scaled drawings, invoice, and put together a new schedule. This was no job for a lush and again I was grateful. Everyone was trusting me with the greatest responsibilities in my life. As the year went by I was geographically moving further east and west, broadening my future political horizons. To prepare myself for retirement, someday, I took two night courses at Oakland University. One course dealt with appraising machinery and equipment and the other course was in real estate. Upon completion of these two classes, I joined the American Society of Appraisers.

The greatest joy after four years of sobriety happened when I was President of the Church Council. We were searching for a replacement of our pastor. A call came from the Synod to interview a recovered alcoholic pastor. I was chosen to see him due to my own personal background. I found the man working part-time in a lower east side gas station in the grease pit. He was performing his pastoral duties in a run down mission half way house. Alcoholism draws no lines on mankind.

After talking and shooting questions at him while he worked, I knew he was our man. Throughout my life I was always willing to give a second chance and sometimes a third to everyone. This pastor was with us for four years and he truly fired up the congregation. He only had one slip and his true abilities started to blossom out. Typical of real ex-alkies, he put all his energies toward goodness.

He was finally transferred to a bedroom community in the suburbs of Milwaukee. They had a serious alcohol and drug problem with their youth, they had $400,000.00, and did nothing. The pastor devised all kinds of programs, activities, and spent their money wisely. He was able to save that church from disaster. He now heads a large alcohol rehabilitation center.

This incident will be memorable for a lifetime — a recovered alcoholic was able to give another recovered alcoholic another chance.

Chapter 19

The Top

The next three years were very busy years. Three additional foreign car clients were added to my territory and I picked up Pennsylvania, New York, New Jersey, Virginia, and Maryland during expansion plans. Iowa, Minnesota, and Missouri were thrown in as bonuses. My real estate career was put aside for a while. Having my eye on national advancement, I ran for AMVETS 4th National District Commander unopposed and was now representing the largest area in total membership in the USA. That put me right square in the middle of my new consulting/survey business — Michigan, Ohio, Illinois, Wisconsin, Indiana, Missouri, Iowa,

Kentucky, and Minnesota. I know the Hand from above was putting these pieces together for a reason.

I criss-crossed the northeastern part of the country working hard and playing politics at the same time. This was the first position in AMVETS that allowed any travel expenses. I coordinated my survey trips for a two-fold purpose. Even though I was self-emloyed, I still had a boss. My orders came from the prime contractor — a mass production sign company in Knoxville, Tennessee. They allowed me thirty days to respond to a survey request. They were also agreeable to my veterans involvement. My immediate boss was also a veteran so he understood and it helped. I addressed him as The General. He always liked that and our personal relationship grew strong.

That particular year I put in close to 100,000 miles of travelling and made dozens of AA talks in various cities. I had two sets of speeches standing at all times. This enabled me to diversify and inject messages useful to various audiences. My AMVETS travel allowed me to establish a beautiful rapport with key people around the country. These new contacts were very useful to me in my later plans.

At the AMVETS National Convention in Florida, I ran against a "team" for National Finance Officer and was badly beaten. The exposure was there and I came back the following year and was elected without opposition. The two years of holding this position enabled me to learn the internal workings of the organization. This was a good stepping stone to get to the big one. Checking the records, I discovered that seventeen national commanders made it to the top from the finance position. In the middle of the year, we switched our original plans and decided to make my big move in Atlantic City, New Jersey. This was one year earlier than originally planned. It turned out to be the wrong thing to do.

For those of you who don't know too much about politics, be it in school, church, union, community, or in clubs, people usually gather in two or more groups. One of these groups is usually a clique or the powerhouse, and they control most elections. We were not any different. Naturally, they had the major appointments to the most influential committees. They usually were able to muster the greatest number of delegates to come to the conventions. It's a very interesting experience. You may wonder at this point why bother to get involved in such heavy politics. When you get to the top of anything, people listen to you. You recall when I joined the AMVETS in 1963 that I saw a lot of potential members to reach out to and possibly help those with drinking problems. This was my ultimate goal.

Supported by the team, we figured I had a good chance of beating my opponent from New Jersey. But we forgot about the geographical advantage my opponent had. At 4:00 a.m., with nobody in the lobby to work on, I was told to go to bed. They told me we had at least a 28 delegate lead and I should get some rest to look fresh for the election. Behold, the next morning a bus pulled up from New Jersey with 34 additional delegates. I lost that election again by only six votes. That number six has cropped up in three major elections for me. But once again there was victory in defeat.

We spent a whole year reorganizing our planning committees. As in the past years, it wasn't necessary to drown this failure in a bottle. Amazingly, this setback refueled my desire. I was optimistically determined to win. We did it in Milwaukee, two to one. I was sober, without the old pseudo-strength that I had so long assumed came from alcohol. Perhaps that was the greatest victory.

Upon assuming office, I was ready with a 13 point plan and a convention mandate for a new AMVETS national headquarters building. Things moved exceptionally quickly and smoothly. I had a valid real estate license and the D.C. crowd ran with the project.

As National Commander, I was invited to a photo session with President Carter and Max Cleland. Zbigniew Brzezinski hosted a dinner and two luncheons pertaining to the Salt II Treaty talks at the White House and I also had the honor of representing AMVETS at these functions. There was a special luncheon at the Department of Transportation at which a Cabinet official presented us with a special citation for outstanding contributions to high school students throughout the nation through out "Driver Excellence" program.

There were special awards from the Department of Labor and the Veterans Administration. Every other week I either received an award for the AMVETS or was awarding someone for their achievements. We planned a weekly visit to Capitol Hill for a half day to keep in touch. I established contact with the Stars and Stripes weekly publication. They gave us tremendous coverage around the country. The Washington Post was good to me. We had adopted the Special Olympics program after a luncheon session with Eunice Shriver, its national chairperson. We were able to assist in a Nazi war criminal investigation with the Department of Justice. With two secretaries and three phones you could really move around, literally speaking. Everyday was one to remember — I kept a daily diary and my picture travel story consists of six large scrapbooks.

I will later touch briefly on my travel to foreign countries. It would take a book in itself to relate all the places I visited, at times accompanied by my wife Ann. On all our major journeys, Ann and I felt awe and reverence at the sites of so much democratic history in our wonderful country. We felt the spiritual presence of the men and women who championed freedom in battles. More than ever we felt truly blessed to be free and to be Americans.

I savored these experiences as would a man brought back from the dead. I was amazed and grateful that I had been granted such a renewal of my life and was able to realize so many goals without once taking a glass of alcohol into my hands. This was the true victory, as I think all recovering alcoholics will agree. TO THE TOP WITHOUT A GLASS!!!

Chapter 20

The AMVET Year

Soon after the installation and swearing in ceremonies, I found myself shaving one morning and stopped in amazement to look at myself. Here I stood, a recovering alcoholic, now the National Commander of a quarter million members and I would represent them around the world. "Fantastic!" In deep humility I prayed to my Supreme Commander above, "You put me here, now please help me."

We had work to do. There was the AMVETS national headquarters building to construct. I told the chairman of the building committee to put on travelling shoes and to find some suitable property in either Washington DC, Maryland, or Virginia. We settled on a beautiful piece of land for $197,000.00 in Lanham, Maryland, about 27 minutes from the White House.

After getting three appraisals on our old building (the highest being $700,000) it was a real challenge with my past real estate experience to barter with the wheelers-dealers in the D.C. area. It didn't take too long to receive a $950,000 firm offer without commission. Of course I had a lot of help — bless them!

The next task was financing the cost of construction. We were able to obtain an 8½ percent loan through county bonds when the prevailing interest rate at that time was 12½ percent. It was all done through an eighteen person building committee, and in a veterans' organization that alone is a miracle as everyone wants a piece of the action, not like in a private project.

It started out as a roomy structure on two floors with a full basement. I personally laid out the floor plans. Over five years have passed and things are getting tighter as we have installed a ¼ million dollar computer system. In addition, the Service Foundation has doubled their business and was bursting at the seams. We still have the 78 car parking spaces. I definitely realize that this project was not all my doing — He held me by the hand. There were some tears as well as joys, but it was a lot of fun and a thrilling challenge.

At the old headquarters, I, as the National Commander, had a studio apartment two blocks away. There were a total of six weekends spent there. At the new facility we planned a three room condo for the Commander with beautiful furnishings. Posts, departments, corporations, and individuals contributed monetarily to make the new building a truly beautiful edifice.

Invitations were pouring in from all over the USA and foreign countries. My executive director and secretary were busy putting together the yearly agenda, trying their best not to create a conflict of interest. My foreign trips to France, South Korea, and the Philippines will be related in more detail in the following chapter.

On the domestic side, the AMVET testimony presented on Capitol Hill in March 1979 was the most memorable to me. An eight man Veterans Affairs Committee in the House of Repesentatives listened to my 18 minute presentation about our concerns. Then the same testimony was presented in the Senate with questions fired by the highest in the land.

Just walking those great halls, meeting those legislators, being so close to the machinery of our political system was intoxicating enough — I certainly didn't need the crutch of alcohol. As my term progressed, these same contacts became invaluable to help others around the country. To this very day I find it a great and special privilege to have this respect and honor. I have never abused it.

There were many social functions to attend two or three times a week with dignitaries from the entire country and the world. I noted the dazzle and mistique of the night life in Washington. It was

different from New York, Broadway, or Hollywood
glamour. People all around were trying to exploit
each other. "Me" was of ultimate importance at the
expense of everyone else. It was truly a world in a class
by itself.

I lived near Embassy Row in D.C. and when there
was a spare moment, I did a lot of foreign visitations,
always receiving a warm reception. I accidentally
chose a church in the area which President Carter and
his family attended regularly. There are many
beautiful churches and buildings in our nation's
capitol and I was able to visit many of them on
different occasions. After the Veterans' Day
celebration at the Amphitheater in Arlington
Cemetery, we attended a very impressive final
ceremony at the National Cathedral. Never will I
forget the click of the heels of the Honor Guard at the
Tomb of the Unknown Soldier and the laying of the
wreath at that Tomb. I get a chill in my spine each
time I think about it.

Visitations to 38 state departments and hundreds of
posts were squeezed into that year. Personal
testimony was presented in Michigan, Massachusetts,
and in Illinois to their state legislatures. I also had the
distinct pleasure of meeting the governors of Iowa,
Massachusetts, Illinois, Ohio, and Wisconsin. Keys
to cities, resolutions, and gifts from dozens of mayors
all over this great country added to the thrill.

Receiving red carpet treatments at airports, city
and town halls, departments and posts was a daily
occurrence in my extensive travels. This included
many interviews on radio and TV and news media

presenting AMVETS views on major concerns and issues. Exchanging ideas with other veteran organizations was part of the agenda. Meeting with top people in labor, transportation, commerce, foreign relations, immigration, FBI and the War College, Pentagon, Secretaries of Defense and the Army was a continuous occasion. There were numerous visits to the Veterans' Administration for an update or for input. There was even a visit to my old alma mater, the Corps of Engineers in Fort Belvoir, Virginia. What a difference in reception after a period of 35 years and a few extra stripes as a civilian. An embarrassment never forgotten was a last minute invitation to participate in a flag burning ceremony in Maryland. I was to be the principal speaker. I have always taken pride in writing my own speeches but now there was no time. One of my staff was a retired colonel so I sent him to the Pentagon to get a prepared speech available from the Speech Writers Bureau. My driver was late in picking me up for the 40 mile trip. Upon arriving we discovered that the agenda had been moved up because of my delay. A brigadier general was reading "my speech" word for word. What a gut feeling. I almost fell off the platform backwards. Talk about fast manipulation of words. No more such crisis for me from now on. I carried two or more speeches to every occasion thereafter.

All my travels were first class, with greeting parties, hospitality suites, food and drink (coffee, that is). They all had been given the signal in advance. This National Commander does not in any way object to drinking except that he himself cannot have one. It was acceptable no matter where I went.

The boys in Texas sure did it up big — like all Texans do. I stayed at the Regency in Dallas in the governor's suite. My agenda included a five day tour of Texas. First it was a box seat at the rodeo in the Coliseum with an introduction to the entire crowd. At the first AMVETS post I was given a $100.00 white cowboy hat with my name embroidered inside. Next they took me to get a tailor made cowboy suit that was ready by that evening. The following day as we moved along I was presented with a pair of genuine lizard boots. Twenty-two lizards went on the chopping block for that pair. Then I received a leather belt with my name on it, a pair of spurs, monogrammed shirt, and a fifty dollar bill with which to light up my cigar. I said no way, so someone lit my cigar with a two dollar bill and I gave the fifty to my wife. Crazy, Man! They wanted to give me a "hoss", but I couldn't get it to D.C. on the plane. No matter where I went, the hospitality was fabulous. Thank you fellows, one and all.

Another tear jerker and very grandoise affair was a testimonial dinner given for me half way through my term of office. Vince Humphries, my campaign manager together with my home post, the Outer Van Dyke Post 27, put on a real show at the Polish Century Club in Detroit. There were wall to wall people, about 400 from all over the state and country. Gifts, resolutions, plaques, and keys from neighboring cities came pouring my way. What a memory! A salute to all of you with deep thanks.

All the state department tours around the country included a visit to the VA Medical Center in their area. One that I particularly remember is the Chilicotte, Ohio facility. As I was to leave through the front door, I stopped dead in my tracks and the entourage behind me almost fell over each other. I overheard a young Vietnam patient talking to his wife on an outside public telephone. He said, "Honey, I feel fantastic — if only I can stay sober after I get home." I had heard about the "revolving door syndrome" many times before.

This incident bothered me for quite a while and I knew right then that I should do something about this in the future. Would you believe that phone call set the tone for my new career in alcohol awareness. You can see the guiding hand right along in my dedication to helping others. It was the first step to a large scale involvement with my fellow drinking buddies. The next big step came the night of my swan song at the National Convention Banquet in Cleveland, Ohio.

Chapter 21

Foreign Travels

Before I wind down my career as National Commander, let me take you briefly on a few foreign trips on which I was privileged to represent my country and the AMVET organization.

PARIS, FRANCE

Annually, the AMVETS National Commander is invited to attend a meeting of the World Veterans Federation. Here representatives from major veterans organizations meet to discuss important community and veterans concerns on an international level. The location changes annually, this year's meeting being held in Paris.

One of the main problems under discussion was the availability of conveniences for the handicapped, among them things such as depressed curbs and toilet facilities. We take many things for granted, but this topic has been discussed all over the world and finally today all new construction requires these conveniences. The veteran is working for all mankind.

The highlight of the trip was the placement of wreaths at the Arch of Triumph by all major organizations. After four days of meetings, we extended out trip to do some sightseeing. We took a bus trip to Marsailles and visited the castle of King Henry VIII, a beautiful edifice surrounded by gardens. Let me just note that the building (barn) housing his 2,200 horses would make better living quarters than his servants had. We stood on the square where Henry the Eighth was finally beheaded.

We took miles of walks in downtown Paris where most of the buildings seemed to be designed by the same architect. From the top of the Eiffel Tower you could see that the layout of the entire city was similar to a hub, with the main streets protruding like spokes from its center. The same pattern exists in Washington DC.

The Notre Dame Cathedral was a dazzling structure inside and out. The city's theater district is like our Broadway in New York. They never close. We went to see the original "Follies Bergere" - it was fantastic, and in the raw. We paid $40.00 a piece for seats in the aisleway and had to sit on the steps. The tourists sure pay the piper. A McDonald hamburger was $3.85. A polka dot Pierre Cardin tie for which my daughter paid $12.50 was priced at $30.00. Arrow shirts started at $40.00. Ladies' boots normally priced here for about $40.00 were selling for $300.00. My wife tried on a pair of boots and asked the salesman the price. When she told him she did not wish to purchase them, he got so mad that he threw the boots clear across the store. You could buy three nice dresses at Saks Fifth Avenue for about $700.00 here, the price of one dress at the finer boulevard stores, but the label is worth three times the value.

We stayed at the Hilton and were really surprised at the antiquated toilet facilities. A car agency around the corner had a 1979 Plymouth priced at $27,500.00 against ours at $5200.00. They hate us. Tariffs are exorbitant. We used subways to get us everywhere and found them to be cheap, clean and fast. Aside from beautiful boulevards, the streets are narrow, dirty, and the people are cold. You can have your dog served at your table even in fine restaurants. There are open markets with meat hanging down from sticks. Bread is carried under the armpit without any wrapping. You don't allow your eyes to wander too far off street level because you'll step into a catastrophe. People were everywhere — like a beehive. Castles a block square are closed down, using one corner for tourists. You would be ushered into four dressing rooms before you came to the main dining room. We even saw the private boudoir of the king's mistress behind the queen's bedroom. All this is a tourist attraction. No one could really afford the maintenance or the servants to keep a castle today. Yes, our trip to Paris was an unforgettable experience.

SEOUL, SOUTH KOREA

My wife and I were hosted by the Korean War Veterans Association, a part of the Korean Government's military umbrella. Everything was first class, the air trip, Regency Hotel quarters, private transportations, meals, etc. All we had to do was sign the tab — real high living.

The first four days were spent attending meetings and sharing many common veteran interests. State luncheons and dinners were a part of our everyday agenda. Meeting the top military and government officials was a constant whirlwind schedule. Speaking to various assemblies and thanking them for the hospitality and cooperation between our governments became a routine — a very pleasureable one.

The most dramatic event was the greatest assembly of warfare equipment marching for two and half hours in a parade review and you are constantly saluting. Most of the military might was purchased by the American taxpayer. We have a very large contingency of troops in that land along with several large bases.

We also have several AMVET posts there. I had received complaints about one particular post operating practically at the front gate of a base. Upon taking a trip to this location, I found out that an American soldier had paid $25,000.00 for a post charter. The Korean government is very strict in their military operations as a whole, but at times they look the other way when it comes to our American camps. They permit veterans organizations to operate night clubs with very lax controls. You can imagine what happens when a shady operator takes over. I pulled his post charter right off the wall and notified the local authorities. The operator came to Washington thirty days later to try to pick up a new charter. I absolutely refused to grant him another one.

Seoul is a thriving city, but their living conditions are no match for even our poorest. There are two classes of people living there — the rich and the very poor. Naturally, the military segments live like royalty. I was amazed at the tailor shops under the sidewalk of main street. There was cheap labor and hand made suits for $40.00. I will never forget the DMZ line — only a few feet to hell. May it never come this close to our shores.

On the final night there was a banquet. I had the honor to speak to a mini-parliament of a province (similar to our state legislature). I was presented with a Medal of Honor by the President of the South Korean Government.

THE PHILIPPINES

This was a royal treatment trip for a lifetime of memories. Upon arriving by first class Philippine Air at the airport in Manila, we walked through a forty man open sword honor guard on a red carpet about eighty feet long. By the way, on all these trips our baggage was handled by special security and whisked unopened through a side entrance into a private club at all airports.

This trip had a fifteen day agenda. All the bus transportation was led by a double police escort.

People scattered like flies in front of us. Hundreds of WWII jeeps converted into cabs roamed everywhere. There was beautiful striping and art work on these vehicles. We arrived at the Manila Hotel and were quartered in the old General MacArthur suite — Gorgeous! Most of our flying from province to province was done in the old C-300 transports. It was fun.

On this trip we had an entourage of 35 AMVETS who came at their own expense. Most of them had served in the Army somewhere in these islands. We started with a welcoming reception by Mayor Bagatsing at City Hall. That night we had dinner in his rose garden with a big outdoor barbeque. He had heard about my love of cigars and presented me with a personalized name band of Cubans in a cedar box with my initials carved on the front. My wife received an expensive full table linen set. All the AMVETS received appropriate gifts.

Every night ended with a state dinner or banquet as we travelled around. At the first banquet I asked the commanding general why there were no women at the head table. He told me that it is military protocol to have officers on one side of the room and the women on the other side. I told him that in America all wives sit next to their husbands. From that night on my wife had a place card at all head tables.

It was a hectic agenda during the entire visit. On a helicopter trip over a particular valley, they made me sit in the middle so as not to get hit by stray bullets from the mountain area. If you go climbing into those hills you may never come back. Guerilla warfare is still prominent outside the city limits.

At one military base we had a briefing around a conference table. I sat on one side of the Lt. General and my wife sat on the other side. We both admired the gold braiding on his hat. It matched my wife's yellow blouse. I was going to ask him for the hat but I figured I would do that after our six hole golf game before the banquet.

Everything had been prepared for the quick golf game. I saw two guards with sub-machine guns standing at attention near our golf bags at the first tee. I asked the General what this was about. He told me that every so often a screwball takes a pot shot at him. The guard walked beside me with an umbrella in one hand and a sub-machine gun in the other hand. You can imagine what that did to my game!

When we came back to headquarters, I saw my wife with this beautiful gold braided cap. Ann said she asked the General and he sent his aide to the quartermaster and that was it. My luck, now when she is mad at me and is wearing this hat in the kitchen I have to salute her on my way to my office-den in the back end of the house. Oh well! It isn't too bad — good memories!!

At one of the large dress parades, I was honored with saluting all the units as they passed in review. Leaving the stand, we drove in a white command car with the commanding general once more driving from unit to unit and saluting. There I was presented with the Cross of Honor.

Outdoor barbeques everywhere — they eat the crispy skin of the animals like we eat potato chips.

The outstanding delicacy is to slurp a baby chick out of the shell. A retired general is now the island commander of the American Legion of 40,000 members. I do have to honestly say that the average veteran is respected there.

Our last night was spent with Major General Fidel V. Ramos, Cammander of all Armed Forces. We were in an outdoor garden having dinner with about 100 people in attendance. I was presented with a silver encased sword — no numbers as to how many lost their heads with that one.

A few minutes out of any city we could see villages of huts on stilts, animals roaming around, and women carrying their pack load on their heads. Poverty was typical in their daily living. GOD BLESS AMERICA ... We have recognized the Philippine soldier who served in the US Army and now have a growing AMVET Department. We didn't see Marcos. He was sick. We did have the pleasure of spending an evening with his wife, Imelda Marcos, at a presidential ball.

Chapter 22

Swan Song

The final days of my tenure as AMVETS National Commander were coming to an end. The staff was busy putting together a seven day agenda for the national convention in Cleveland, Ohio. There were last minute preparations for guest speakers, a two tier seating arrangement for the head table, awards to be given out to local and foreign dignitaries, and all the rest that goes with putting on a national veterans convention. A good executive director and master of ceremonies made the details easier.

I handled the day to day business of the convention with very little problem. This event usually makes or breaks your year. We had attained 12 of the 13 personal goals for my year, and the results were good, as attested in the committee reports. A last minute creation of AMVET JOE, a membership vehicle that was designed by me and presented to the delegates for adoption. It was a new type of recruiting poster and is still being used today.

The Saturday Night Commander's Banquet rolled around quickly. This is the most celebrated affair for the National Commander — also his swan song. Eight hundred and thirty-one people were in attendance, 244 from my home state of Michigan. Naturally, there was an hour long cocktail party before the main event and picture sessions with the honored guests. We were then assembled in a side room of the banquet hall in preparation for escort to our seats at the head table.

Mingling with all the dignitaries, I spotted Max Cleland, then Chief Administrator of the Veterans Administration, sitting in his wheelchair. I ambled over to him and once again my Higher Power took over and spoke. Without any previous planning, I told him point blank that I was an alcoholic. I told him that there were some things I had noticed in my nation wide visitation of the VA facilities that should be changed. In five minutes I nearly told him my whole life story. He said he had a personal interest in the alcoholism problems of our nation, especially of the veterans. He was well aware of all the alcoholics around because he had to dodge them in his wheelchair upon entering his apartment complex. During the winter they would sleep on the grates in the sidewalks. Steam from the boilers below them kept them from freezing. He said, "Ted, I wish I had known you three years ago. We could have done some great things together." On parting, he asked me to call him Monday morning. Once again I moved a step closer to my veteran/alcoholic goal. Talk about being at the right place at the right time.

The entire evening program was a grandiose affair. I received the highest VA Administrators Award from Max Cleland. I got up to make my swan song, as they call it. I had prepared very careful notes for that finale and again it was not me talking. From the very beginning, I thanked everyone with heartfelt gratitude for allowing me this great privilege to represent them around the world and for the wonderful year of accomplishments. Then I made a public testimony of who I had been and how I got there. I made an eighteen minute speech that I could not believe until I heard it on my recorder. There were some that knew me, but most of my audience didn't. As I talked, you could have heard a pin drop on the carpet.

That was the end of my anonymity. Everybody now knew and I felt a great load fall off my shoulders. I hope you will understand my attitude for revealing myself in this book. I had to be honest with myself. I had never experienced such an accolade — over three continuous minutes and then hundreds of people came up to congratulate me. Once more I felt free — they accepted me for what I am.

To put frosting on the case, Patricia Hughes, then editor of the Stars and Stripes, asked me to write some articles on alcoholism after I got out of office. She also suggested that I should write a book — and that's how it all started. She told me later that she had alcohol problems within her family. She thought a column on this subject could reach a lot of veterans who could be helped. I was in a new kind of business — the kind in which I wanted to be.

It was a dramatic weekend for me. I couldn't rush through Sunday soon enough to make my Monday morning call to Max Cleland. At precisely 9:00 a.m., I asked my secretary to put the call through. He had been waiting for my call. We were both on the same train of thought. He asked me how soon I could come to his office for a brief discussion of a plan that he had in mind. My driver had gone down to the post office and I could be there within the next half hour. The Veterans Administration main headquarters was located on Vermont Avenue, about twenty blocks from our office.

Upon arriving at the building, I was announced to his secretary by the downstairs receptionist and in a few minutes I was going up to Max's floor in his private elevator. All of this excitement alone put my nerves on edge as I was ushered into his private inner office. It was surprising to see the simplicity of the decor of this inner sanctum.

Our conversation began where it left off the night of the banquet. He told me about his friend, the former Senator from Iowa Harold E. Hughes, who was a recovered alcoholic and who had written a book with Dick Schneider entitled "The Man From Ida Grove". Hughes left the world's position of power to be a servant of Christ as an evangelist and counselor.

Max had just purchased a hundred copies of Hughes' book and he gave me one. He asked me to read it and to give him an honest insight. He said he hoped reading this book might give me some ideas for the future. He was indirectly telling me to write.

Then we got down to the purpose of this meeting. Max wanted me to make an overview of the alcohol and drug programs in about a dozen VA facilities around the country. That type of survey was a new approach, as I was to find out later, because it was from a layman's standpoint. Max's administration was to expire in December 1979 and there wasn't much time left to put together a program of substance. I was to get in touch with his Deputy Administrator, Rufus Wilson, who happened to be a friend of mine and from my home state of Michigan. Rufus was also a past national commander of AMVETS. He would make the preliminary arrangements for my future travels, expenses, etc.

I had daily prayed for guidance all these years and I knew that this direction was a part of His master plan for me. There was no doubt in my mind but to blindly follow this new inner feeling. What an opportunity to do something for my fellow veterans. What an opportunity to make a difference!

Chapter 23

VA Tours

After the national convention in August 1979, I had two weeks to tie up all ends of my tenure and to clean out my desk. There were a lot of farewell parties. Never once did I have that desire to bend an elbow for alcohol.

Arrangements were already underway to make a visitation to two of the Michigan VA Medical Centers in Allen Park and Battle Creek. In the meantime I was appointed as Chairman of the AMVETS Drug and Alcohol Abuse Committee. This helped me along on my next step to help my fellow veterans. This also put me in the driver's seat to establish a column in our bi-monthly newspaper.

This is when and where the title of the column and of this book were born.

I was immediately able to pick up my subcontract work with Plasti-Line, Inc. and went back to the same territory as if I had never left them a year ago. They had been very good to a recovering alcoholic and they never knew it until recently. I am forever grateful to all of them.

My daily schedule had picked up so much momentum that I seemed busier now than I ever was during my commandership. But I knew that the key to happy sobriety was to keep very busy. I dashed out the first column and mailed it to the National AMVET and the Stars and Stripes publications, both based in Washington, DC. That was the launch of my new writing career. The wheels were also spinning to eventually attempt writing a book. Constant research and note taking were a must for my new living pattern.

Only three and a half months remained to do the overview contract of fourteen Veterans Administration Medical Centers. A new President was taking over and all the top slots were filled with new people. My first visit was the VA Hospital in Allen Park, Michigan, only a few miles away from my home in Warren. I had been going to this facility for over twelve years as a volunteer. This was a new ballgame for me to deal with the top administrators and doctors.

All my scheduling was done out of Washington, DC with a predetermined agenda submitted by each medical center director. I would fly into a city, pick up a rental car, and arrive at the hospital to a red carpet treatment and a dozen people greeting me at the door. Each visit started out with a half hour staff meeting and numerous introductions. The VA system is a complex one consisting of 140 hospitals, 27 outpatient locations, domicile and nursing home care, and a total capacity of about 80,000 beds. It is a big business, so everything must be done with a tight control.

The first hour was spent looking over the hospital's specialized equipment and other amenities. Some hospitals were geared for special treatment care while others were more generalized. Let me tell you that I have never seen such modern tools for medicine. Our veterans truly have the best equipment available for their needs.

Getting "nosey", I found out that about 26% of all VA beds at that time were taken up by alcohol or drug abuse patients or related illnesses or diseases. I have also recently learned that this figure is true in private hospitals as well. Thinking about these figures helps us realize the scope of our nationwide alcoholism problem.

After looking over all the fantastic equipment, the next step was to have a meeting with the chief of staff. Most of them are excellent — down to earth and caring, loving human beings. The stigma of alcoholism still showed up during some of our conversations. Most, however, were deeply concerned and very helpful.

I was then assigned to the doctor and personnel in charge of the drug and alcohol wards. They were usually separated in different wings. Some of the patients were in sad shape. Most of the medical centers had a de-tox area consisting of 8 to 10 beds for the "baddies" as we call them. We went from bed to bed visiting and asking a few questions. I would sneak into the latrines and get a lot of information that I wanted right "from the horse's mouth" as they say. Mostly all the responses were good and patients spoke favorably about the VA facilities.

There were many therapeutic classes run. Everything was run very professionally, but also casually. Around noon we had lunch and I usually sat down with one of the counselors. They knew what it was all about and I found out information I would never receive up front. Every hospital has its share of recovering alcoholics working where they could fit best. I was told many times that they made the best employees. They understood the problem and knew how to handle it better.

At one of the facilities I spent the first hour in admissions to see what procedure was followed if someone had just came off the street. I even witnessed a typical drive up ambulance case. It was a terrific learning experience from a purely layman's standpoint and I will cherish and respect that experience. One doctor in particular admitted that they themselves are learning about the disease and the treatment of alcoholism. Unfortunately, at that time, medical schools only spent about two hours covering that subject.

In general, the VA program consists of a 30 day stay with some hospitals having an extended period if necessary. But when funds are cut in the budget, everybody down the line suffers and I was told that unfortunately that part of the hospitalization program usually gets the ax first. They have many kinds of activities planned for the patients and there are even weekend passes if they are deserved. There are a few that always abuse the privilege. Every hospital has Alcoholics Anonymous meetings in the evenings once or twice a week. I was privileged to talk on four different occasions and enjoyed being a part of them. At this point I should remind you that I had gone to private hospitals twice for treatment during my binge days. This gave me an overall compassion and comparison and I knew what to look for. You may recall that my hospital stays didn't help me because I stubbornly couldn't admit my failure at social drinking.

There was a good after-care program devised for patients after they left the hospital, but it was quite expensive to run. This program consisted of having outside counselors in certain areas where discharged patients could go and get further help. Some of the patients have to travel long distances to get help in hospitals. They lose touch and hence the "revolving door" syndrome. The VA has extensive outpatient clinics on the drawing boards, but that takes millions of dollars before they could ever become a reality. That is the key to after-care: reaching out into the patient's community together with the helping hand of the Alcoholics Anonymous.

The VA also has a family co-op unit that works with the wives, children, and other family members of the patients. This is very important to recovery. National statistics show that an alcoholic affects three and a half other people around him or her. To develop and expand these programs takes big bucks which we can never seem to find until it's too late. The entire VA system has a very good drug and alcohol treatment program. Some even have extensive job placement opportunities and most have good rehabilitative projects.

In three months I was able to overview the VA facilities in Michigan, Ohio, Illinois, Wisconsin, Texas, and California. They were all very good, but the ones I visited in Ohio were the most outstanding. I made out my report just as I found things, holding nothing back. This report was presented to my superiors in Washington and to the Hon. Max Cleland. Sixteen recommendations were submitted with the report and I understand that some of them were utilized. Then we ran out of money again. I am deeply appreciative of this great challenge. I almost decided to take up medical courses at night school.

Pounding the fast track schedule that I had set for myself, my resistance was at a low ebb and I developed hepatitis-B somewhere on the road. They had no medicine for it then and the doctors gave me a 50-50 chance of recovery and three months to do it considering my age. The doctor told me to lay in bed for eighty days.

"Don't disturb the liver," he said, "it is up to you and God." I told the doctor that we would give it a good try. I also told him that I often communicate with my Supreme Commander. Prayer was the key. I used to tell God that I was ready, but if He had an unfinished job for me, I'd like to hang around a while. I wanted very much to write this book. I wore out six pairs of knee pads praying, and it sure worked.

Chapter 24

The Alcoholic's Children

It was rather difficult for me to ask my three children, after forty years, to share a chapter on their feelings about an alcoholic father during their growing up days. I knew it opened a lot of healed wounds, but we all feel better about it today. Their unedited comments are written here.

PATRICIA

Dear Dad:

When you asked me to express my feelings about how I felt growing up with an alcoholic father, I underestimated that task. I'm finding all kinds of emotions surfacing. Many things that I've tried to remember have been blocked out. Time has healed all the hurt, frustration, and anger. Nevertheless, I will try my very best.

Your drinking caused our lives to lose a very important thing to any child, and that is stability. Thank God that Mom and Babcia (Polish for Grandmother) provided that. I really didn't appreciate it then, but it all makes sense now. I felt a tremendous responsibility for the family when you were drinking. In some ways, I felt personally responsible for your drinking. I thought, "What am I doing wrong to cause my dad to drink?" It was often frustrating to come home from school. I kept wondering whether you would be drunk or sober when I got home.

The holidays were the worst. Most times it was hard for you to stay sober and what should have been a happy time for a kid was not. On a few occasions when you were sober, I felt such great joy and excitement that I cannot describe it. We were a "family" then. I wanted to hold onto that time forever. I would ask God to let this be the last time you would drink. However, it wasn't. It continued on for so many years.

It was hard for me to understand why Mom didn't leave you and take us away from it all. It would be so simple. Just pack up and go. Where? I didn't think that far ahead. Many times I would get angry at both you and Mom. Why did she let this happen? She was there to protect us when you were drinking. I now see the great burden she carried for so long and am grateful she hung on the way she did. Today we are still a "family" because of it. I'm grateful to my dear Babcia, your mom. Without her providing us with shelter and food many times, I don't know how we would have made it.

We never had a home of our own. I guess this bothered me a lot. We moved so many times that it was hard to have any friends. If I did, I had to be careful about bringing them home, not sure of you and not wanting to be embarrassed. Not you personally, but what condition you'd be in. When you were sober I was so proud as any daughter would be. I would tell my friends, "My Daddy is a painter and could play the violin. He is such a good looking man and can whistle like no one else." But when you weren't sober, I felt bitterness, anger, and hatred, all the things I despised.

I was confused with my feelings toward you. I was brought up to believe you love your parents no matter what they do. Why then, did I feel this way? I couldn't make sense of this at twelve years of age. Even when I first married and started having my own family, I still had trouble dealing with it.

We've come a long way since then, a whole lifetime, it seems. I'm grateful we're a family. I forgive you for all the bad times. I realize now that so much of it was not your fault! I thank my Mother for being so strong and loving. I think I found out today for the first time where I got my strength. I thank you for teaching me to persevere, not to lose faith.

You've come a long way, Dad. In doing so, you have earned my respect, you always had my love.

GLORIA JEAN

Thinking back over forty years is a long time. Many things happen in a lifetime, some good and some bad. Some things you wish you could forget. But I guess psychologists say you can't forget your childhood, and they are absolutely right.

So I'm just going to put down on paper some thoughts about me. My name is Gloria but my family has always called me Jeannie. I'm the second or middle child of Ted and Ann, right between my sister Pat and younger brother Teddy. I think I was always stuck in the middle. I never did figure out if that was a good position to be in. I do know that I always felt out of place as a kid. To top it all off, I had to live with a father who had a "problem". This in turn, gave me problems.

My Dad's problem was alcohol. He was an alcoholic. All of my life at home my Dad drank. As a little girl I remember my Dad coming home drunk and my Mom and him fighting over money. My Mom needed this money to feed us or to pay some bills. This happened often. How I hated it! I would cry myself to sleep at night and say a child-like prayer, "God, when I grow up, don't let me marry someone who drinks." God heard that prayer and answered it.

Thinking back, I remember how I would never want my friends to come over unless I knew my Dad was sober. Many times I'd come home from school and find him sleeping it off so he could go out again. Sometimes I would come home and he would be working. Maybe this would last a few weeks. How I wished I it would last forever, but he would always start again.

I remember specifically an incident that happened when I was in high school. This was during one of Dad's drinking bouts and he was heating himself something to eat on top of the stove. We had a gas stove and the food was in a glass dish. The dish cracked and broke from the heat. He told me to clean it up and I refused. I told him he was the one who was drunk and used too much heat and caused the dish to break, so he could clean it up himself. Needless to say, he got very angry with me. He picked up a piece of the broken dish and held it close to my face. He told me he would use it on me if I didn't listen to him. I told him to go ahead if he wanted to because I didn't care. Then he just threw the glass across the room, swore at me, and went to bed. I was so mad at him at that time and hated him for what he was doing to our family. Why couldn't I have a father like the other kids had?

Other things I remember were living in Dearborn, having no heat in the winter, splitting one can of sardines for the family's supper, Dad spending time in jail, a Goodfellow Christmas, fights, drinking, shame, not being sure if my Dad would be sober for my graduation, not having things like other girls had ... I know there are many more things in my memory, but I chose to leave them lost. I also remember people being kind to us and my Mom. I remember my Mom doing her very best for us always, no matter what the circumstances.

Just before I was to get married, my Dad was on one of his drinking binges again. I told him if he didn't stop, there was no way I would walk down the aisle with him. He stopped before the wedding, got himself back into shape, and walked me down the aisle. Thank you, Lord.

It seemed his drinking was getting worse. There was nothing anyone could do. Not long after my marriage, less than a year, I became a Christian, a born-again Christian. Now I could really pray for my Dad. My life was now different. His drinking got worse. Dad just wasn't going to stop. He thought he could "handle it". I kept praying somehow God would help him. To tell you the truth, I wasn't even sure God could help him, but I prayed anyway. In the meantime my brother got into some trouble and we brought him home to live with us.

One day God answered my prayers. My Dad joined AA and really stopped drinking. I couldn't be more proud of him. I'm also very proud of my Mom who stuck by him through everything. I'm grateful to her for all she did for us kids as we grew up under the worst of conditions sometimes.

That part of my life is past and I don't dwell on it. I guess in a way it has made me what I am today. I'm not bitter or angry. It has helped me to be more understanding of someone with a drinking problem. I can feel compassion for their family; I've been there.

We can't change our past. I really had no choice in it, but I can use things that happened to me to make me a better person. I hope and pray that this "better person" can help make this world a better place for someone.

TED

The memories of my childhood are not the greatest
on which to look back, which is why I usually don't.
Most kids can look back with fond memories on the
excitement they had, the vacations with the family,
the picnics together, the happiness that is usually
there as a family.

In my case, it was different. I don't really remember
any family vacations without yelling and screaming.
On our frequent trips to Harsen's Island, we would
usually stop at almost every bar and wait in the car for
my father. The times our father did something
together with other families, I would wonder how
long it would take for my father to have too much to
drink, start arguing with my mother, and embarrass
us all. Most arguments would end with my father
leaving for the bar and with my mother in tears.

I tried not to talk too much about my family. Most
kids would tell about the things they did over the
weekend, but I kept quiet. I would go to my friends'
homes and their fathers were always there. They
would joke and talk with us. I longed so much for a
relationship like that, one they took for granted. I
never invited my friends to my home because I never
knew if my father was sober. I didn't want to walk
into a bad situation.

At the age of 14 I started resenting my father for
what he was doing to us. I dreamed about what I
would do when I got older. I would take my mother
away and support her and give her the things she
never had. In school, I knew I couldn't afford much so
I never went anywhere. I felt my clothes were not

adequate, but they were clean. I remember going to bed at night with toothaches so bad I cried because there wasn't enough money to see a dentist.

I remember the different homes we lived in and the cramped quarters we had and the rooms I had to share with my sisters. In one house we had to put mattresses on the floor to sleep. I knew I could never have friends sleep over like other kids did. I wondered when we would have to move again because our rent was overdue. We would go to another new neighborhood and have to make new friends. I became withdrawn so I wouldn't have to make new friends and then try to keep them away from my house. I remember one Christmas in Dearborn when the Goodfellows delivered our food and presents because we had none.

I became very close to my mother, hoping she would always be there. She became both my mother and father. What would happen to me if something happened to her? I feared for her safety and tried to protect her. I know my sisters resented me because we were so close, but she was all I had.

I did have one friend as a child, and that was my grandfather. I spent lots of time in the basement cooking and helping him down there repairing shoes and fixing things. Every Saturday we went to the lumber yard and picked up boards and nails. He did things with me that I couldn't do with my father.

One of my happiest memories was when my mother decided to leave. She went to stay with my older sister and I moved in with my younger sister. She didn't stay long, but I stayed until about a year after I graduated from high school. I could finally have friends over without fear of embarrassment. But I was still concerned about my mother's safety.

I try not to look back because it's not very pleasant. I can look back now and see that I am a better person because of it. I hope I am a better husband and father than I might have been. Today I can say that I love my father which is something I could never say as a kid.

Chapter 25

Outreach

In the past five years I've renewed my participation in AA groups that I used to attend regularly. Several opportunities for making talks have come my way, and I've responded enthusiastically. Going back to those meetings, I feel like I never left them. That is what AA is all about — the fellowship and the friendship.

Since I was the National Commander, the Junior AMVETS youth group has invited me several times to be the principal speaker at their annual banquet at the national convention. I was asked to speak about alcoholism four out of six years — a real honor. That has been one of the greatest rewards, to be recognized as a helping hand to their problems.

I continue to write my columns in the National
AMVET, Stars and Stripes, Vietnam Vet News,
Oklahoma American Veteran News, Texas AMVET,
as well as free lance stories. I keep busy answering
letters from around the country. With a circulation of
about a quarter million, there is a great potential for
reaching out. I have finally come one step closer to
reaching and achieving my master plan, that of
reaching out.

Today I can speak freely without any reservation
about alcoholism in any kind of gathering and am
accepted for what I am. It makes no difference
whether it is in my American Society of Appraisers
meeting, my church or any other church, at the Polish
Century Club, an AMVETS function, PLAV (Polish
Legion of American Veterans) meeting, a Lion's Club
gathering, or any other function. The name of the
game now is OUTREACH.

Over the past years I have made many speeches on
many different topics to many different audiences.
Here is one of my favorite speeches, one that
addresses teenagers and alcohol. In over four years of
outreach efforts, I consider the following article to be
one of my more meaningful contributions:

TEENAGERS . . . THE NEW ALCOHOLICS!

Society's newest alcoholics are teenagers! Do you
know where your children are? Do you know what
they are doing? Drinking has been with us since the
beginning of time, but a new epidemic is creeping up
on us in the 80's.

In 1960 drugs came on the scene and alcohol became square. A 1960 FBI crime report showed 13,537 drunk driving arrests under the age of 18. In 1970 it was 31,173 ... more than double. The shift swung back from drugs to alcohol. The horrors of marijuana and heroin overshadowed alcohol problems for a while because of emotions aroused in parents and other adults.

Alcohol is now replacing drugs to the extent that it is the number one problem . . . it is a drug. Young people at odds with society around them are shifting to alcohol to get "high" whereas years ago they drank to be "smart" and to show they were grown up. Heavy drinking and even alcoholism is showing up among children 14, 13, 12 years of age and younger.

Nearly 50,000 young adults ages 15 to 24 die in the United States each year. If all the diseases that kill them were eradicated, 40,000 would still die. Violence, not disease, kills them. Car crashes, other accidents, murder and suicide, in that order, account for almost 80% of the deaths in this age group. A large proportion of these violent deaths have a common factor: alcohol. Alcohol is involved in about half of all traffic fatalities and other accidental deaths among young people, one fourth of murders, and along with other drugs in about a third of suicide among the 15 to 24 year olds.

All drinkers are not drunks. Only about 9.6% of 95 million drinkers are problem drinkers. It is most prevalent in the 21 to 24 year old age group. Within this age group, 55% of the alcoholics are in the lower income level, 25% are in the higher income groups.

Why do teenagers drink? It seems to be more acceptable by adults. Questioned about their first drink, many stated it was taken at home, approved by their parents. Others started with their friends ... do you know who their friends are? It is very important. Drinking started way back with most ethnic groups. With the Jewish, it is a part of religious practices several times a year. People in Italy and France have wine on the table at mealtimes. There is a low rate of alcoholics among Jews, Chinese and Italians, yet they drink as much as the French and Irish who show a much higher rate of alcoholism. Among Kentucky mountain people, it's an accepted practice. About half of junior and senior high school students in seven counties showed unusually heavy drinking. Forty-five percent admitted destroying property while drinking and 28% were injured or arrested.

Why drink? Teenagers claim they drink for social reasons, expression of adulthood, to bring down anxiety, because of pressure of their friends, drinking friends, problems, availability, rebellion against parents, as well as other factors. There are many reasons why young people drink. The big question is why are there so many problems with their drinking? One major problem occurs in particular when drinking and driving. The majority of accidents and deaths on highways are due to drinking.

Can you blame heredity or chemistry? No sir! Not if these young people are well balanced and self controlled. Young alcoholics are much more emotionally disturbed than are average adult alcoholics. Early signs of dependency develop very rapidly. Alcohol releases hostility — difficulty in coping with problems. Amnesia, morning and solitary drinking, and prolonged drunkeness suggest psychopathic factors in their make-up. Such youngsters are different from social drinkers.

Again, it matters not what you drink or how much you drink, but what it does to you. Some parents encourage the intake of beer or wine instead of marijuana or other drugs. What a mistake! What can be done? There is no easy answer. Prohibition by law was a historic failure. Prohibition by parents induces rebellion. Treatment is readily available now. Alcoholics Anonymous is now taking in more younger members than ever before. Alanon is for spouses and Alateen is for the troubled youngsters — give them a try. It really and truly helps.

Parents who wish their children to abstain must themselves be abstainers. They must set an example. They must explain the injury to health, damage to brain cells, internal organs, the accidents, and deaths that result because of alcohol intake.

If you drink, drink for pleasure, not to show off. Let alcohol be a part of your enjoyment of food, people and other good things. The plain and simple fact is that every time we are drunk we indeed overdose on a drug because alcohol is a drug.

RULES FOR PARENTS

1. Watch your drinking the way your children watch it — set an example.

2. If you condone drinking, start teenagers to drink at home. Make drinking a casual family pleasure, not a secret self indulgence.

3. Tell teenagers why people drink ... for good fellowship. It is dangerous to drink to escape problems.

4. Point out the dangers of alcohol. Degradation and illness will not scare them, but denying the use of the family car will make them think.

5. Show a film or attend a lecture or a group discussion on drinking where there will be a question and answer period.

6. Get closer to your kids. Attention and love are the best ways to keep them out of trouble, including over drinking.

7. Get expert help! If it's a drinking problem, contact the National Council on Alcoholism, AA, Alanon, or Alateens. Hospital treatment is also available. Look in the Yellow Pages. Take it from me — I've been down the pike. Remember, you don't have to drink to be a success.

The above is just one of my many columns and speeches on alcoholism, just one of my many efforts to reach out. My future plans for outreach call for an extensive lecture tour to youth groups, alcoholic groups, and non-alcoholic groups, as well as more writings.

Epilogue

· · · I had to find much pain in alcoholism before sobriety came to me. It was not an easy road at first.

. . . I had to undergo a complete personality change. I always used conditions as an excuse to drink never realizing then that we have to change ourselves to meet conditions.

. . . I had to make a choice. The choice was to keep on drinking into my own destruction knowing that I was powerless over alcohol, or come to believe that a Power greater than myself would restore me to sanity.

. . . I was willing to admit and accept my failure in drinking and turned over my life to my Supreme Commander above as I understand Him.

. . . I took a very hard and long look at myself and asked to be forgiven for all my shortcomings.

. . . The many years of "hard living" hurt a lot of people and I am still trying to correct these defects of characater and trying to make amends to all of them — one day at a time.

. . . In my daily meditation and prayers, I ask only for His will and to live my life more fully, to be able to give more and more of myself.

Since my sobriety over twenty years ago, it has been my sincere desire to carry this message of my failures and successes to everyone. I am truly and humbly grateful to be able to share my experiences with you.

My avenue to sobriety was through involvement with the programs of a veterans organization. Admittedly, a veterans organization may not be for everyone. All organizations, however, have worthwhile programs to which people can dedicate themselves. Get involved — give of yourself. Only through giving of yourself can you realize your own worth, your own dignity, and your own place in life.

My story is only one of millions that have been shared around AA tables everywhere. No story can help more than letting you know that you're not alone. Help yourself ... admit and identify yourself with this story.

By reading this book you have just attended your first AA meeting. You have heard my story, NOW IT'S YOUR TURN...

P.S. This last chapter was completed under the same apple tree — only 22 years later.

"TO THE TOP"
without a glass

Order Form

IF NOT FOR YOU ...
   FOR YOUR FRIEND/RELATIVE

- -

(Please Print)

WARREN BOOK PUBLISHING CO.
P.O. Box 1376, Warren, MI 48090-0076

Please send me "TO THE TOP" without a glass.
I enclose my check or money order for $7.95,
plus $1.50 postage and handling. (No Cash or C.O.D.)

NAME _____

ADDRESS _____

CITY_____

STATE, ZIP_____

Michigan Residents Add 4% Sales Tax (32¢)